ALL THE PAINTINGS OF
PIERO DELLA FRANCESCA
VOLUME FIVE
in the
Complete Library of World Art

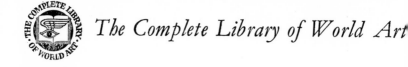

The Complete Library of World Art

ALL THE PAINTINGS OF

PIERO DELLA FRANCESCA

Franceschi

Text by PIERO BIANCONI

Translated by PAUL COLACICCHI

HAWTHORN BOOKS, INC.

Publishers · New York

*Printed in Great Britain by
Jarrold and Sons, Ltd, Norwich*

CONTENTS

PIERO DELLA FRANCESCA

Life and Work

Je hais le mouvement qui deplace les lignes
Et jamais je ne pleur et jamais je ne ris.

BAUDELAIRE

NO other artist's fortunes illustrate the changes in taste better than those of Piero della Francesca, a true "monarch of painting in his time," later ignored for centuries, and then gradually and inexorably restored to his rightful greatness. Only a hundred years ago the critic Burckhardt, in his *Cicerone*, put Piero among the followers of Squarcione: Cavalcaselle, though he was the first to understand him, called him a forerunner of Ghirlandaio, if only for his manner of projecting shadows. It has been said many times, and rightly so, that the artists rather than the critics contributed to his resurrection, and in fact no other classical painter could have contributed more than Piero to the *avant-garde* tendencies of the end of the last century and the beginning of this one, when rigidly formal, rather than romantic, experiences were sought.

Now that his reputation and prestige have been firmly re-established, the critics have been interested in defining— among other things—the relationship between the master's artistic and theoretical activities and the chronological order of his works. By these means they hope to trace the history of his complex artistic development.

One should not take Vasari too seriously when he writes that Piero della Francesca began life as a mathematician ("Piero studied mathematics as a boy, and, though he was induced to become a painter when he was fifteen, he never deserted the study of that science . . ."). It is now generally assumed that his theoretical treatises belong to the latter part of his life. Even so, it has not been easy to dispel a common suspicion that for him science prevailed over imagination. Berenson, who understood Piero's art better than most, wrote: "At times you feel him to be clogged by science." This suspicion lasted for a long time until it became clear that perspective and mathematics in his paintings have both a lyrical and a personal value. They are essential elements of his pictorial language and thus enable him to achieve a greatness and majesty that have never been equaled. It was a long time before Longhi's splendid definition of Piero's painting—*sintesi prospettica di forma-colore* ("a synthesis in perspective of form and color")—which makes him the immediate forerunner of the Venetian School, was accepted as one of the current ideas of the history of art.

There are many differences of opinion about the time-sequence of his paintings. This is due to the fact that as a painter, Piero did not show marked changes in his development. As far as his media of expression were concerned, his art revealed from the beginning a remarkable assurance. He never had the beginner's awkwardness and his style remained unchanged after his stay in Rome in 1459. His perfect world appears immutable and this explains why there can be so few doubts about the works attributed to him. One should add that Piero worked very slowly: it took him seventeen years to complete the *Misericordia* altarpiece, fifteen for the *St Augustine* and only a little less for the

Arezzo frescos. His works, therefore, do not follow one another in time but are often parallel and interconnected—which does not help the historian. One does notice, however, a progressive detachment from the creative process which in the artist's last years was replaced by theoretical interests. A significant observation was made by Nicco Fasola in noticing that very few theories from Piero's *De prospectiva pingendi* were passed on to his paintings. One may go even further and remark that those theories were taken from pictures that he had already painted and used as examples of applied perspective. Furthermore, his last works —not the early ones—contain some evidence of evolution: the Brera altarpiece (plates 162–9) suggests a move towards new tonal subtleties, very much *avant-la-lettre*, immersed as it is in an almost sub-marine kind of light, while the *Nativity* (London, National Gallery, plates 156–61) shows a more tender and informal approach, a form of naturalism which critics have reasonably attributed to Flemish influences.

Piero was a placid man, inclined toward meditation. It is therefore reasonable to imagine that his thoughts matured slowly: his painting never gives the impression of warmth or passion, but recalls, rather, the calm attention of the master craftsman. At times, indeed, he showed a craftsman's indifference to the type of work he was doing: he accepted commissions for altarpieces involving a gilded background, he repeatedly allowed others to contribute to his works, sometimes leaving them to complete whole sections of a painting. This last actually happened in the case of his first commission in his home town, Borgo San Sepolchro. In the San Francesco choir he placidly followed the traditional method of painting all his principal scenes on the same plane, without showing any of the perspective bravura accomplished earlier by Mantegna in the

Ovetari Chapel. The progress of his work is visibly marked by the role he alloted to his assistants. We can almost imagine the artist lost in thought on the bridges over the Arezzo, while his pupil Lorentino was busy weakening his master's sublime cartoons and another assistant, Giovanni da Piamonte, was industriously replacing the hairing on the heads of the stately characters with lifeless little snakes.

The lack of information about Piero della Francesca's works is matched by the total absence of those facts or quotations that might convey a picture of the artist as a man. Vasari's biography tells us next to nothing. It is, however, difficult to imagine him as a proud man—someone has written, "he had the pride of a king, of a creator God." On the other hand, Vasari appears equally ridiculous when he calls him "a kindly old man." He must certainly have been a withdrawn personality, enveloped in his searching meditations. But he was basically a son of the soil, not at all removed from practical matters: he was a councilor in his native town, the prior of a religious Order, a house- and landowner. He loved life in the full sense of the word.

It is satisfying to know that the Friars of St Augustine rewarded him for his work both with money and with land. It seems he never married, nor had children. We like to picture him as a man of few but sound words, and deliberate in his gestures—typical of both the cautious peasant and the subtle courtier, who can be said to represent the two extremes of human nature. From his preference for the barest essentials in word and gesture sprang perhaps the archaic quality of his art, for it always seems distant, almost primordial. I would not agree, however, with Lionello Venturi when he states that Piero used an ironic approach in his work in order to mitigate his peasant-like admiration for luxury and magnificence. I cannot see how a man of his integrity and classic simplicity could have experienced such a dualism in his artistic work.

The discovery by Gaetano Milanesi in 1856, that the artist was in Florence in 1439 and that he worked there with Domenico Veneziano, is of the utmost importance with regard to Piero's artistic formation. It gives insight into his complexity by enabling us to understand that Piero della Francesca, born in a locality mainly influenced by Sienese art, was educated in Florence—in one of the greatest periods of that city's artistic splendor—side by side with a painter of Venetian origin.

How old was he in 1439, as he walked across the bridges of Florence with his friend, Domenico Veneziano? We do not know for certain, nor do we know what he had done before that time, since this is the first piece of documented evidence about him that has been handed down to us. He was born at Borgo San Sepolchro, a highly civilized, if small, country town, that has been rightly called the heart of Italy. His father was a tanner. Vasari—who must have been well informed about him, and took pride in recording that Piero was a friend of one of his ancestors—gives the date of his birth as 1406, but it now appears that this date was about ten years too early. The Florentine document discovered by Milanesi states: "Piero, the son of Benedetto, of Borgo San Sepolchro, is with him [Veneziano]." This does not enable us to establish what the relationship between the two artists could have been—whether one was the master and the other the assistant—nor does it justify the assumption that Piero was very young. His name does not appear again in the payments made to Veneziano until 1445. It would seem safe to assume that Piero arrived in Florence, not before the age of twenty, at a time when new ideas, launched and defended by Brunelleschi and later set down in writing by Alberti, had been transformed into live art and had found substance in the Carmine frescos and in Brunelleschi's architecture.

In his treatise, *Della Pittura*, Alberti showed that he had fully understood the importance and the value of the new generation of artists, in whom he acknowledged "an intelligence inferior to none of the most ancient and famous masters." It is very likely that Piero frequented the circles mentioned by Alberti, though, if he did, we can well picture him, as always, sitting in a corner listening discreetly but saying little. But the fact that he was a member of that group and had drunk at that particular source of intellectual fervor should be interpreted as one of the essential factors of his artistic formation.

It is worth noting, on the other hand, that Vasari did not include Piero's name among the impressive list of those artists who became famous through the study of Masolino and Masaccio's frescos in the Church of the Carmine in Florence. But young Piero della Francesca must have been as attracted by Masaccio's virile energy as by Masolino's pinks and tender greens. These were then to be seen, clear and luminous, on the walls of the Brancacci Chapel, and even more so upon the vault and lunettes. Not only did Piero have an extraordinary gift for assimilating a pictorial language previously unknown to him, but he also had a formidable capacity for absorbing all facets of style and composition; an infinite number of pictorial experiences appear to converge in him. Gentile de Fabriano's rich embroidery on the draperies in the *Adoration of the Magi* must have enchanted him as much as Masaccio's fresco of the *Holy Trinity* in the Church of Santa Maria Novella. Piero remembered the chromatic narrations of the Late Gothic style and the radiant, almost sensuous, caress expressed in those paintings. He pruned the crowded compositions of the so-called "International Gothic" style, eliminating from it all that was ineffectual, replacing it with an intellectual three dimensional positiveness. Yet at the same time he preserved something of its original innocent gentleness. This, of course, had already been partly done by Fra Angelico and by Domenico Veneziano, not only in Florence but, according to Vasari, also in Loreto. Nor should one forget the influence of the Sienese School, at that time dominant in the upper valley of the Tiber. In Arezzo the boy Piero must have admired Lorenzetti's polyptych in the Church of Santa Maria della Pieve and later, Sassetta's altarpiece in the Church of San Francesco at Borgo San Sepolchro. Chledowski, the art historian, also includes among the artists who influenced Piero della Francesca the modest Domenico di Bartolo. The more one amplifies and complicates the list of Piero's antecedents, the less one runs the risk of exaggeration.

Having presented him with her magnificent inheritance— her artistic *milieu* and her world of art treasures—Florence was to figure no longer in Piero's life. It seems highly unlikely that he ever returned there. Three years after his mention in the document previously cited, his name reappears in the official records of his home town, where he was appointed a town councilor. Three years later, in 1445, the Company of the Misericordia gave him his first recorded commission, a great polyptych to be executed against a golden background. We must assume that he did not undertake this conservative venture with any particular zeal, for a short time later we find him traveling along the Adriatic coast to Ferrara where, about 1448–9, he met Roger van der Weyden and was thus able to study at first hand various Flemish works, and also paintings by Pisanello.

Unfortunately, no trace is left on the walls of the Ducal

Palace at Ferrara of Piero's frescos—even by Vasari's time they had disappeared. However (and Sir Kenneth Clark also notes this in *Piero della Francesca*, Phaidon, 1947) this visit to Ferrara was of lasting importance not only to Piero but also to north Italian art, for some of the eminent *Quattrocentisti* (fifteenth-century artists) of the Ferrara School reveal his influence both in tonality and architecture. Nothing remains of Piero's work either in Pesaro or in Ancona, but in 1451 he signed a fresco at Rimini. This fresco was executed in the Church of San Francesco, rebuilt by Alberti as a temple in honor of Prince Sigismondo Malatesta. The year before Piero had painted a small panel, now in Berlin, of *St Jerome doing penance*. This may be one of the "very beautiful small figures" which, according to Vasari, were painted for the Court at Urbino, one of the places frequently visited by the artist. As we have noted, Piero did not go back to Florence: his art had become too dissimilar from that of the Florentines. The latter were now working wholeheartedly to achieve "mobility of form." Piero della Francesca was, on the other hand, moving steadily towards a formula that would require the human figure to be caught and imprisoned within the static perfection of geometry.

The *Misericordia* polyptych (plates 1–11), the contract for which is dated 1445, must have been executed very slowly, if the last payment was made, as I believe, in 1462. The slow progress is also confirmed by its lack of organic unity. Critics have now agreed on which parts were done by the master and which parts he delegated to his assistants, whom he used freely. Theirs are the predella stories and the smaller Saints painted upon the lateral pilasters. Efforts have been made to establish the probable date of execution of each separate section. The two Saints on the left, *SS Sebastian and*

John the Baptist (plate 6) call to mind Masaccio's plasticity. The same is true of the expressionistic *Crucifixion* (plate 10), and the dramatic gestures of its figures (plate 11)—altogether foreign to the composure that Piero had still to acquire. On the other hand, the two Saints on the right (plate 7)—*SS Andrew and Bernardino of Siena*, the latter was not officially canonized until 1450—are treated quite differently, in a manner very typical of Piero della Francesca. This is even more true of the center panel (plate 1) in which the Virgin's outspread robes call to mind one of Bramante's large architectural niches. The observer is struck by the Virgin's awe-inspiring immobility, and exalted by the fervor of her worshippers. Of the Madonna's face (plate 5) Sir Kenneth Clark has written: "Piero's subtleties of tone reveal a shape remarkably like that of the finest Congo masks in the balance of convex and concave." This he qualifies however: "this head is in no way a mask. We never doubt that its formal consistency will continue all round, and it is a shock to realize that we shall never see the back."

This polyptych was Piero's first documented work, but the first picture which he signed was the Berlin *St Jerome doing penance* (plate 12), a small panel which is unfortunately only partly his own work. It is dated 1450 and the parts he painted himself reveal great chromatic beauty of a strange silvery quality. Its theme reappears in the Venice panel, painted after the Berlin work, which depicts *St Jerome with Disciple* (plate 13). This painting is enriched by a subtle harmony of grays, browns and purple-reds. The mottled landscape is framed by a yellow and blue sky stretching away beyond the hills and seen through the leaves and branches of the tree at right. The Saint's figure, set against the towers of a distant city (Borgo San Sepolchro), has an intensity almost precocious.

The same type of landscape strewn with towers appears in the *Baptism of Christ* (plates 14–22), possibly painted at the same time if not slightly before *St Jerome with Disciple*. This is one of Piero's finest works; we find here the same crystal-clear quality of the air, and the various species of trees, placed in careful perspective, lend a strong impression of distance. The arrangement of the characters reveals an untroubled sense of symmetry, of quiet order, of respect for plane, which we shall find again in Piero's great masterpieces in Arezzo. Note the perfect balance and harmony in the relationship between Christ's smooth body and the marble-like quality of the tree-trunk: then look at the contrast between the unkempt appearance of John the Baptist and the rapt concentration of the three splendid Angels on the left—Longhi described them as "young oak trees sprung from the earth."

The background of *St Jerome with Disciple* is for the most part repeated in the *Baptism of Christ*—or vice versa. The arrangement of the *Baptism* may be found again in a fresco in Rimini's Tempio Malatestiano (Church of San Francesco): the fresco shows a profile of Sigismondo Pandolfo Malatesta kneeling before his Patron Saint, with two greyhounds behind him, against a background "with fanciful simulacra of marble, jade green swags of leaves with coral fruit and a profusion of lapis blue" (Sir Kenneth Clark); (plates 23–7). The conception of the picture is definitely a laic one since the Prince's clear-cut profile dominates the whole scene. The Saint's figure is balanced by Rimini Castle, flooded with sunlight, seen through the round window at right, and by the two enchanting hounds, one white, one gray, facing in opposite directions (plate 27). Although badly damaged, the fresco still has intense chromatic beauty in the few places where the colors have not faded: in the Saint's flesh, in the gray drapery which shows between his legs and in some small details of the Oriental carpet. The date of the painting, 1451, coincides with the probable presence in Rimini of Alberti. This must have been an encounter of vital importance for Piero, whose architecture strongly recalls Alberti's style.

We have come to the highest point of della Francesca's art. The acme of his perfection was reached in the Urbino panel of the *Flagellation of Christ*, in which the Albertian architecture is all-important (plates 28–32 and color plate I). This solemn work is governed by the inflexible laws of perspective. The incomparable dignity and beauty of the human figures standing four square in well-defined spaces; the unerring precision of the formal and chromatic relationships —of a subtlety never equaled since: all these combine to make this Piero's most accomplished masterpiece. Delicate pink-grays and greens in the pearly light at left provide contrast to the intense colors of the figures at right. The work is a perfect marriage of intellectual precision and lyric emotion.

If, subject to circumstances, we were compelled to sacrifice all of Piero's works except one, my choice would be this small picture—to my mind one of the highest expressions of human genius. One should, in addition to its great lyrical beauty, note the bold composition, the violent break in the planes from right to left. The enigmatic presence of the three men on the right (plate 30), strangely withdrawn and reserved, are an excellent example of that confidence in one's station that was typical of Piero's unchanging world—a world whose beings remain untouched by any sentimental anxiety. No one knows for certain who the three men are, though few would question the traditional identification with Oddantonio, Federico's half-brother, killed during a popular rising in 1444, who stands between his two evil counselors.

Piero's *Flagellation* was fairly near completion by the time he undertook and carried out the chief work of his career: the frescos in the Church of San Francesco at Arezzo. But let us first mention another of his paintings of the same period: the *Madonna del Parto* (*Madonna in Childbirth*), a fresco in the chapel of the country graveyard at Monterchi (plate 33). It is an unforgettable experience. The ancient village is only reached after miles of dusty roads, and a long climb to the summit of the small hill, encircled by the wall of the cemetery where one is confronted with a forbidding gate which yields, however, at the pressure of a hand. In a corner of the deserted place stands the closed chapel. A silent woman, armed with a long bamboo stick, appears from nowhere to open the chapel and, once inside, to draw back a curtain on the wall. Immediately her speechless, sullen gesture is repeated with cheerful animation by two Angels on the wall, holding back the curtains of the ermine-lined pavilion, to reveal a brooding, contemplative Virgin, delicately indicating her pregnancy through the parted front of her robes. There is a porcelain blue coldness about this impassive representation of imminent maternity— an Egyptian or Chinese quality—that makes this Virgin akin to the *Madonna of the Misericordia*, but also pre-Christian. Indeed, she is as ancient as time itself. The *Madonna in Childbirth* fresco has a world of its own, but it is a world that cannot be captured on the crowded walls of museums and art galleries.

In the Arezzo cycle the story of the True Cross frescoed on the choir of San Francesco, Piero della Francesca's art reached its full maturity. The work dates over a period from 1452 (the year of the death of Lorenzo di Bicci, an old-fashioned Florentine artist to whom the work had originally been entrusted) to 1466 when a document in praise of the artist mentions the completed work. The choir's vaulting was almost entirely decorated when Piero began work, but the walls were bare. He divided the frescos into long horizontal scenes placed one above the other—the traditional Tuscan method. He distributed his episodes with an eye to composition rather than to the chronological sequence of events: the result was a magnificent epic poem (see diagram on page 47).

On the two lower sections of the east and west walls he depicted two vast battle scenes: at right, a solemn victory parade (*Triumph of Constantine*, plates 74–82), and at left the victory of Heraclius over Chosroes. Upon each of the two upper sections he painted two great aulic events side by side, the one against a landscape and the other against an architectural background: both unified by the fact that they are seen from the same viewpoint.

On the right-hand lunette above the walls Piero painted two scenes depicting, beneath a great tree, the origins of humanity. On the lunette at left is a scene of adoration, divided in two by the tree of the Cross: we witness here the progress of mankind from Sin to Redemption. On the lower part of the window wall he painted two Annunciations: the Annunciation to Mary in full daylight, and the Annunciation that occurred during the night to Emperor Constantine. Above the window are two minor episodes, *The Burying of the Wood* at left and at right a trial: on the lunettes are two solemn prophets.

I think that one should accept Sir Kenneth Clark's theory that the whole work of the Arezzo frescos was subject to one major interruption: initially Piero painted the wall on the right, which is more luminous and shows the least amount of collaboration; then, reserving "for himself the subjects which interested him most", he painted the wall on the left, where the colors are much duller and the intervention of his assistants much more obvious. Between the two periods, according to Sir Kenneth Clark, Piero had gone to Rome, a journey which the Vatican recorded as having taken place in 1459.

In the lunette portraying the *Death of Adam* (plates 34–43), the scene on the right (plate 35) is marked by unusual gravity. In it Piero departs from his usual practice in order to confront us with various types of humanity: aged Eve, the patriarch facing her, the girl in a black stole, and the naked young man, leaning, like a Greek statue, on his crook. All these figures are astonished at finding themselves confronted with Death. The left-hand scene, on the contrary, is one of tremendous excitement: observe the Impressionistic gestures of the screaming woman—a rendering which must have caused a sensation at the time (plate 37).

The two great scenes that make up *The Queen of Sheba and her Retinue* (plates 44–61), in a setting reminiscent of the Urbino *Flagellation*, present their many figures in rhythms that are slow and majestic, in undisturbed areas of color, that prove once again Piero's great respect for mural surface. One may observe here that Vasari never applied to him his recurrent accusation: "making holes in the walls." In this case the artist reverts to his impersonal style, doing away with the previous presentation of different types of humanity: the effect of the whole relies upon the supreme elegance of the figures, on their majestic stances and on their absolute dignity. Observe how frequently the artist makes use of the same attitudes and forms, at times even using the same cartoon reversed—a practice severely criticized by Leonardo da Vinci who, only a short time later, wrote: "It is a very great fault on the part of a painter to portray the same movements and the same fold of drapery in the context of the same story, and to make all the heads resemble one another." We have here two contrasting theories, worlds apart from each other: Leonardo da Vinci's passionate and dangerous interest in psychology and Piero's sublime display of form, a display that attains miraculous heights and in which—to quote the poet Leopardi— "sentiment is really the soul, not the matter of discourse." It would be difficult to imagine anyone who could have expressed deeper feelings more effectively than Piero della Francesca, or a greater adoration and reverence. His is a language in which are perfectly blended geometrical theory and a sense of life, an understanding of the functions of space and sincere human emotions.

It is not only the method of reversing the same cartoon which suggests that Piero della Francesca's artistic language is fundamentally a feeling for pure form, for architectural rhythm, for the almost musical repetition of a theme— with all the variations that a musical theme entails. The quasi-literal reproduction of scenery on the section of the wall opposite the Queen of Sheba frescos and the sections depicting *The Discovery of the Cross and Proof of the Cross* (plates 86–97) confirm this. The backgrounds of these two sections are schematically the same: a landscape at left (plates 44 and 45, 86 and 89), and architecture at right (plates 44 and 54, 86 and 92). Subtle similarities can also be found in the continuity of rhythm and in the clever distribution of the cast around a number of magnetic centers. The figures in *The Discovery of the Cross* (plate 87) are aligned along a curve which is repeated by the hills in the background. The identical semicircular formation occurs close by in *The Proof of the Cross* (plate 92), where the figures are grouped round the kneeling Empress, the focal center being the dead man's body rising from under the slanted Cross— emphasized by a shaft of light. This is not a trick of perspective but a means of linking the kneeling group with the three grave Oriental figures standing at right.

Note the ladies in Empress Helena's retinue (plates 93 and 97): the uniformity of their type, their regular features and large bulging eyes confirm again the fundamental elements of Piero's art as architectural regularity, balance of masses, pulsating tension, and formal interest—as revealed by the great uncluttered circles, like orbits around stars, on the marble façade of the temple. This exclusive and formal knowledge, blended with deep feeling, is all expressed in a picture which Longhi has so rightly described as "natural as any weighing scene at a city's gates."

This blending of aulic gravity and popular simplicity is equally obvious in the minor scenes, marred though they are by others' work: the *Torture of the Jew* (plates 83–5) and *The Burying of the Wood* (plates 62–3). These are both magnificently inventive. In the *Dream of Constantine* (plates 70–3) we find the magic of Italian art's first nocturnal scene. The Virgin in *The Annunciation* (plates 64–9) is one of the most beautiful examples of the "columnar" figures which are so typical of Piero. The etymological relationship between figure, column and cornice is perfectly clear. The whole scene strongly suggests the artist's interest in heraldry. One might almost imagine him to have served his apprenticeship under a painter of escutcheons. *The Annunciation* is divided into four quarters, with each figure centered perfectly within its own rectangle: God the Father (plate 65), the Angel (plate 66), the window (plate 68), and the Virgin (plate 67) —remote and somewhat haughty as are all Piero's women.

The master's heraldic taste is again displayed in the

banners seen above the two battle scenes: in the *Triumph of Constantine* (plates 74–82) their movement, together with the raised lances are enough to convey the victorious elation of the imperial forces (plates 76 and 78), and the anguish of Maxentius' routed army escaping beyond the river (plates 79 and 82); beyond description are the radiant beauty of the pale blue sky, the silver-lined clouds, the pearly light that envelops the glorious scene. The serenity and tranquility, the deep lyrical emotion of the whole picture (color plate II), remind one of Corot, whose work often reflects Piero's infinite capacity for creating essential forms steeped in light.

The *Defeat of Chosroes* on the opposite wall (plates 98–105) is more crowded and seems to lack fundamental rhythmic inventiveness. It is also the more dull by its execution, due for the most part to Piero's assistants. But the *Exaltation of the Cross* (plates 106–13) in the lunette above, though mostly the work of helpers, reveals wonderful inventiveness of rite and liturgy: its balance and rhythm are expertly organized around the central vacuum, made the more evident by the bizarre display of the figures' Oriental head-dresses.

The contrast between the two prophets on the window wall is very marked. The young prophet on the right (plate 115) is one of Piero's noblest creations, but his companion on the left (plate 114) is so crudely painted that one doubts if Piero had any part in its painting. Sir Kenneth Clark attributes this figure to Giovanni de Piamonte.

The same might be said of *St Luke the Evangelist* in the Basilica of Santa Maria Maggiore, Rome (plate 119). Piero was recorded as being in Rome in 1459. There are further records of his lost works in the Vatican, but it is a fact that his stay in that city had no appreciable influence on his art. The journey interrupted his work in Arezzo, but in the same period he was carrying out other commitments. Among these, probably, were the *St Mary Magdalen* in the Duomo of Arezzo (plates 120-1) and certainly the San Sepolchro *Resurrection* (plates 122-5), described by Vasari as Piero's finest painting. It undoubtedly reveals all his greatest qualities: the landscape of this work has a cosmic grandeur and against it the figures seem more exalted than the architectural features. The composition is spectacular in its clarity and is perfectly balanced on the two sides of its central axis. At the same time it reveals great freedom in the juxtaposition of the group of soldiers in the foreground and in the trees silhouetted against the sky in the cold light of dawn. Piero's intuitive understanding of Nature was the greatest of his century.

In 1454 Piero signed a contract with the Chapter of the Church of San Agostino in San Sepolchro for the High Altar's polyptych whose many parts are now being slowly identified (plates 128-32); he must have received the commission for the Perugia polyptych (plates 133-41) not long after that date. These works progressed slowly, and one must admit that in both works the artist's genius revealed itself only intermittently. Most of the work was carried out by his assistants. But in a few major figures, such as the *Saint* in the Frick Collection, New York (plate 129a), the *St Nicholas of Tolentino* in Milan (plate 129b), and in the enchantingly popular stories on the Perugia predella (plates 139-41), Piero not only recovered his original greatness but revealed daring innovations.

So little is known about his life that his movements are impossible to trace. We know, however, that his constant focal point was his home town, where we find him in 1467, engaged in public service, after having received a commission from the Company of the Annunciation of Arezzo for their new banner. This work he carried out during the following year at the Villa della Bastia, where he had gone to escape the plague in Borgo San Sepolchro.

In 1469 he paid a brief visit to Urbino, to see the panel upon which he was to paint a Last Supper for the Company of the Corpus Domini. The Company, however, later gave the commission to Justus of Ghent—but paid ten bolognini (approximately two lire and fifty centimes) to Giovanni Santi for hospitality extended to Piero during his stay in Urbino. Santi—who was Raphael's father—was later to mention his guest in his *Rhymed Chronicle*, in a verse which also included the names of Masaccio, Andrea del Castagno, Paolo Uccello, and the two Pollaiuolos. However, Giovanni allowed Piero only a chronological eminence:

> *Piero del Borgo antico piu' di quelli . . .*
> *Piero of Borgo, older than all of these . . .*

We may console ourselves with the knowledge that his son derived a greater profit than he from Piero's work.

Perhaps it was on that occasion, and certainly in Urbino, that the artist once again marshaled his powers in order to paint the double portrait of Duke Federico da Montefeltro and his Duchess, Battista Sforza (plates 142–7). The two portraits form a diptych, painted on both sides: on the reverse of the panels the Duke and Duchess are seen in their triumphal chariots (plates 148–51). In addition to the remarkable pictorial beauty of the painting, one should note here Piero's capacity for using pure form as a means of expression. It is doubtful that anyone has ever more forcibly conveyed the sense of domination, of possession, of absolute mastery, as Piero did in Federico's portrait. Everything is remarkable in these pictures: the warts on the Duke's face (plate 147), the pearls around Battista's neck (plate 144), the landscape "of shining lake and gentle hills, enveiled in mist" (Sir Kenneth Clark); the minute dots of distant trees (plates 145 and 146), the conditioning of the light from the left which emphasizes the Duke's rocklike, somber profile; the Duchess's face, lit frontally, which has the quality of old and rare ivory and is almost the same tone as the sky. Even more radiant are the *Triumphs* on the reverse.

The Senigallia Madonna (color plate IV and plates 153–5) reveals a completely different pictorial technique. Here nothing shines. All is dim, and the architecture in the background represents a total departure from the solemn Albertian style previously followed by Piero. We may still find this in the Williamstown *Madonna and Child with Four Angels* (plate 152). The gray and asymmetrical background of the Senigallia picture is an innovation, and so is the device of sunlight filtering through glass—clearly a Flemish influence. The human figures, too, are rather strange, less geometrically severe. Longhi has aptly described them as: "the sacred elephant's little eyes of the angels . . . and the obese, lymphatic Child."

Some Flemish elements are also to be distinguished in the London *Nativity* (plates 156–61), a picture which indicates a new attitude marked by a gentler sentiment. We see a regretful and surprisingly humble Madonna (plate 159), an unexpectedly realistic braying donkey, charming determination in the music-making Angels (plate 157), realism in the magpie and the tufts of grass upon the roof of the hut. The beautiful mottled landscape at left (plate 160) evokes the magic of Piero's early panels.

The altarpiece in the Brera, depicting the Virgin and Child surrounded by Angels and Saints, with Federico da Montefeltro kneeling at her feet (plates 162–9), is one case where Piero appears to have rediscovered his true expression—that "pictorial appetite" which Sir Kenneth Clark considers to have declined with age and with the master's new interest in theoretical speculation on perspective and solid geometry. The harmony achieved between the static figures and the coffered barrel vaulting of Bramantesque design in the background, the behavior of light directed at exalting the spacial impression, the spellbound suspense of the group, liturgically assembled under the mystical perfection of an ostrich's egg; the refined pictorial subtleties and sub-marine tonality, the Duke's shining armor, the long thin hands of the Saints (so different from Federico's which were not painted by Piero)—all in this sublime panel speak a language not to be heard again for centuries. Here Piero della Francesca reaffirms that supreme dignity is to be found in immobility, in pure existence; that gesticulation is vanity; that his characters are instruments of expression in his hands, not actors expressing themselves; that truly great is he who contemplates mystery with steady eyes, without fear, having conquered and stilled forever all feverish passions; that the road to be followed is one of absolute geometrical perfection and order. In fact, these are the very same principles that, with the decline of his creative urge, Piero set forth theoretically in his mathematical treatises. Here he translated into clear, scientific formulas all his fundamental and constant intuition and which sealed his paintings with a truth understood with absolute certainty, with no fear of error or trickery. It was, in fact, a sublime world, touched at times only by the cold shadow of perfection.

That this art was destined to be ignored until Cézanne rediscovered it (*Traiter la nature par le cylindre, la sphère, le cône, le tout mis en perspective . . .*) over four hundred years later, appears to us now inevitable, if one thinks of the direction taken by Tuscan art: the psychological approach,

Leonardo da Vinci's romantic *sfumato*, Antonio Pollaiuolo's interest in anatomy. All these were opposed to Piero's tendency to match the human figure with the perfection of geometry and to place it within the immobility of perspective. This is well illustrated in that notable view of an ideal city, *Architectural Perspective* (plates 172–3), which I believe is correctly attributed to Della Francesca. It disturbs one to think that worlds as far removed from one another as these could have been in fact so close during the artistic fever of the second half of the Italian Quattrocento—the more so if one considers that that particular period exhausted artistic experiences which could have lasted for centuries. It was therefore inevitable that the rediscovery of Piero della Francesca's art was due not so much to his few direct successors as to Venetian and modern art, to those who, reacting against Impressionism, turned to the severity of Cubism.

Of his last years little is known except that in 1482, when he was nearing seventy, he was still in good health, for he rented a house in Rimini. In his last will and testament, dated 1486, he is stated to be seventy years of age and sound in mind and body. Some notes about his will, written in his own hand, would refute a reference to his blindness made by Marco di Longaro. On the other hand, the image of an old blind artist led by a small boy through the streets of San Sepolchro is one that attracts the biographer. If Piero was indeed blind, we may comfort ourselves with the thought that he would have treasured the mental picture of a supremely ordered and luminous world, a picture so beautiful that he did not regret the loss of his physical sight. At the time of his death, October 12, 1492, he was buried in the Church of the Badia, San Sepolchro, with the honor he deserved by the Brothers of his Company.

APPENDIX ON THE THEORETICAL TREATISES

No study of Piero della Francesca's art would be complete without some mention of his treatises, especially those concerned with optics and perspective. These two problems had already been tackled by Ghiberti and Alberti, but they lacked Piero's careful mathematical approach. His search for scientific precision was perfectly in tune with the ideals of the Renaissance and it was not long before the artist's written works acquired a considerable reputation. Luca Pacioli recalls that Leonardo da Vinci abandoned his plans for a book about perspective as soon as he heard of Piero's treatise; in 1506, Raffaello Maffei from Volterra mentioned the treatises with profound admiration, and in 1569 they were extensively quoted by Daniel Barbaro in *Pratica della prospettiva*.

In recent years critics have established beyond any doubt the existence of three books by Piero della Francesca:

De prospectiva pingendi is about "commensurateness, which we call perspective", which is one of the three parts of painting, for according to Piero "painting consists of three parts, called by us drawing, perspective and coloring." This book was probably dedicated to Duke Federico of Urbino, as one may deduce from the dedication of the *Libellus* (see below) to his son, Guidobaldo. It would therefore appear to have been written before 1482. Two manuscripts of this treatise are in existence: No. 1576, in the Biblioteca Palatina at Parma, the text of which is written entirely in Italian, and is in Piero's hand, as are the drawings; and Codice Ambrosiano C. 307 inf., in the Pinacoteca Ambrosiana at Milan. This text is in Latin, translated by Matteo dal Borgo and is written in the hand of a transcriber, but the corrections and the drawings are by Piero. The best edition is that by G. Nicco Fasola

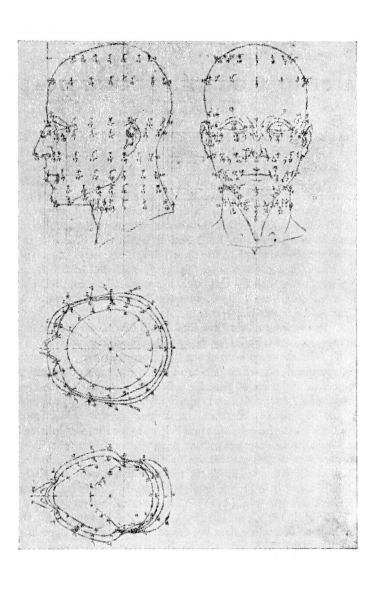

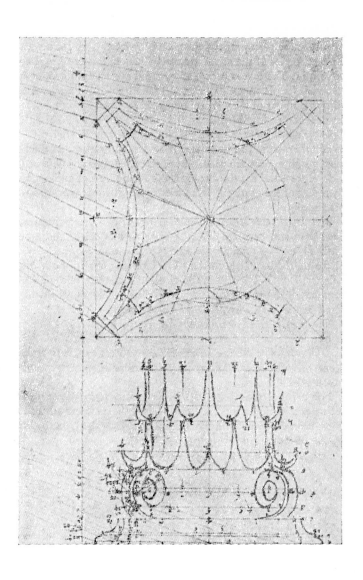

(Florence, 1942), in two volumes, the second of which consists of forty-nine plates reproducing seventy-nine original drawings. Two examples of the drawings can be seen in this book on pages 30 and 31. The text is preceded by a full and useful introduction in which Fasola states: "In this treatise Piero della Francesca sets forth a number of theories on perspective which are complicated by ever-increasing difficulties. The artist does this in order that, having solved these initial problems, he may later find the solution to all other ones. The work is divided into three parts: in the first part, plane figures are placed in perspective, as are solids in the second part, and the third teaches the same forms of construction by means of the more empirical methods used in the workshops of his time."

The *Libellus de quinque corporibus regularibus* was written at a later date and "so that his [the artist's] wits might not soften with disuse"—as he wrote in his dedication to Guidobaldo, Duke of Urbino. It is in the Cod. Urbinate 632 in the Vatican Library, Rome. The text is the work of a copyist, but the drawings are in Piero's hand. It was published by G. Mancini in *Rendiconti della R. Accademia dei Lincei* (Rome, 1915).

There is a third manuscript by Piero, called *Del abaco* and is numbered in the Laurentian Library in Florence, Cod. Ashb. 359. Written for the use of merchants and traders, it is a short work on commercial arithmetic, algebra and geometry, and is profusely illustrated.

For a fuller treatment of Piero's writings and those of his follower and plagiarist, Fra Luca Pacioli, the reader is advised to consult an extensive and most useful essay on the Quattrocento by A. Guzzo in *La Scienza* (Turin, 1955).

BIOGRAPHICAL NOTES

1415–20. Piero, born in Borgo San Sepolchro (today San Sepolchro), near Arezzo, the son of Benedetto de' Franceschi, tanner and shoemaker, and Romana di Perino da Monterchi. Vasari stated that he was born in 1406 but the date is unlikely to have been much before 1420. It is not known why he was commonly known as "Della Francesca."

1439, SEPTEMBER 7. The house of charity of Santa Maria Nuova in Florence pays Domenico Veneziano for his frescos in the Church of Sant' Egidio. The document records that "Pietro di Benedetto from Borgo a San Sepolchro lives with him."

1442. He is appointed town councilor in his native San Sepolchro.

1445, JANUARY 11. The Company of the Misericordia at San Sepolchro commissions a polyptych from Piero (see comment on plates 1–11).

1448–50. He works at Ferrara.

1451. He signs the fresco in the Tempio Malatestiano at Rimini.

1454, OCTOBER 4. The Chapter of the Church of St Augustine at San Sepolchro commissions from Piero, *pictori presenti*, a polyptych for the sum of three hundred and twenty florins (see comment on plates 128–32).

1459, APRIL 12. In Rome, he is paid the sum of one hundred and fifty florins "for part of his work on certain paintings that he is executing in the Chamber of His Holiness [Pope Pius II]" (see under Lost Paintings).

1462. Marco di Benedetto receives "the sum of fifteen scudi in part payment for the panel painted by his brother Master Pietro" from the Company of the Misericordia, probably for the polyptych commissioned in 1445.

1466, DECEMBER 20. The Company of the Annunciation of Arezzo commissions Piero to paint on a banner (now lost) "the most beautiful picture that is possible." The Company recommends that "the heads of Our Lady and of the Angel be gentle and beautiful and their faces angelic." The document confirms Piero's worth as an artist by stressing the fact that he is the painter of the "principal cupola" in Arezzo (meaning that he was responsible for the frescos in the choir of the Church of San Francesco).

1467. At San Sepolchro, engaged in public activities.

1468. Piero goes to Bastia to escape a plague epidemic and there "he finished painting the above-mentioned banner" for the Arezzo Company. On November 7, the Chamberlain and two monks collect the banner, having paid the balance of twenty-two gold florins and take it back to Arezzo where the whole Company "praised it highly for its great beauty."

1469, APRIL 8. The Company of the Corpus Domini at Urbino pays to Giovanni Santi, Raphael's father, the sum of ten bolognini "for the expenses of Maestro Piero dal Borgo who has come to see the panel in order to paint it." This was probably the panel for which Paolo Uccello had painted the predella in 1467, and which was eventually entrusted, in 1474, to Justus of Ghent (who, however, "did not do his duty"). The panel portrayed the *Institution of the Eucharist* (Urbino, Ducal Palace).

1469, NOVEMBER 14. The Chapter of the Church of St Augustine pays him, partly in money and partly in land, for the panel commissioned in 1454. This is almost certainly the polyptych which is now being identified and reassembled (see comment on plates 128–32).

1471, FEBRUARY 23. Piero fails to pay taxes owed to his *Commune* (borough).

1473. A document by proxy states that he is living in San Sepolchro.

1474, APRIL 12. He receives payment for the frescos painted in the Church of the Badia at San Sepolchro.

1478. He paints a fresco of a *Madonna* (now lost) for the Company of the Misericordia at San Sepolchro for a fee of eighty-seven scudi.

1480–2. He becomes Prior of the Company of St Bartholomew at San Sepolchro.

1482, APRIL 22. At Rimini he rents a house with a garden and a well from a gentlewoman, Giacosa, the widow of Ganimede Borelli.

1486, JULY 5. His last will and testament is drawn up by a notary, Ser Lionardo di Ser Maria Fedeli. In the document Piero is described: *In extremo actatis suae calculo*, but *sanus mente, intellectu et corpore.* A sheet of paper signed by Piero, containing his notes for his will is kept in the State archives at Florence. It reads: "I wish to be buried in our church and in our family tomb. I leave to the church itself ten lire, and ten lire to the Company of the Corpus Domini, and ten lire to the church's Madonna. Of what remains I leave half to my brother Antonio and if he dies before me, to his male sons. I leave the other half to the heirs of Marco, that is to say, Francesco, Bastiano and Girolamo and as they die may it pass from one to the other."

1492, OCTOBER 12. From the register of deaths in San Sepolchro: "M. Piero di Benedetto de' Franceschi, a famous artist, on October 12, 1492; buried in the Badia."

1556. Berto degli Alberti tells what he has heard from Marco di Longaro: "The said Marco, when he was a small boy, used to lead by the hand that excellent artist Master Piero di la Francesca who was blind. This he told me." But Piero's blindness could only have occurred in his final years, as proved by the notes on his will which he wrote down and signed in 1486.

PIERO DELLA FRANCESCA'S
PAINTINGS

THE MISERICORDIA ALTARPIECE

(Plates 1–11)

Panels, 273 × 323.* San Sepolchro, Pinacoteca Comunale. The altarpiece consists of the following parts (see plan on next page): in the center the *Madonna of the Misericordia with Eight Donors* (*arched panel, 134 × 91*), and above it *The Crucifixion* with the *Madonna Addolorata and St John* (*panel, 81 × 52·5*); at left of the central group *St Sebastian* (*arched panel, 108 × 45*) and *St John the Baptist* (*arched panel, 108 × 45*); above them are *St Francis* (*panel, 54·5 × 21*) and *The Angel of the Annunciation* (*panel, 55 × 20·5*); at right of the central group, from the left, *St Andrew* (*arched panel, 109 × 45*) and *St Bernardino* (*arched panel, 109 × 45*); above them *The Virgin Annunciate* (*panel, 54 × 21*) and *St Benedict* (*panel, 54 × 21*). The commission for this work was given to Piero on January 11, 1445, by the Company of the Misericordia at San Sepolchro, on the condition that he finished it within three years. The altarpiece was to be *deauratam de fino auro et coloratam de finis coloribus et maxime de azurro ultramarino*; another condition was *quod nullus alius pictor possit ponere manum de penello preter ipsum pictore*. Furthermore, the artist was to inspect the painting regularly for ten years after completion, and to repair

any deterioration that might occur. This precaution, one assumes, was taken because of Piero's technique of mixing oil with distemper, after the practice of his master, Domenico Veneziano. The polyptych, which was damaged by fire and, in the seventeenth century, inserted in a heavy Baroque frame, was taken apart in 1807 when the Company was disbanded. It was reassembled without the frame in 1892 and transferred to the Palazzo Comunale at San Sepolchro. The polyptych is in bad condition: in places it was repainted to restore damage by the fire, and part of the gold is new. Piero, we know, did not respect all the clauses of the contract. In many parts the collaboration of assistants is very obvious, and most critics believe he did not paint the small lateral Saints and the five predella stories. (These are attributed by M. Salmi to Giuliano Amidei and by other critics to an unknown Florentine painter. Only H. Focillon accepts the authorship of Piero and at that, is influenced by Fra Angelico.)

The execution of the altarpiece must have taken a very long time, as shown by the changes in style in the different parts and by the fact that the figure of St Bernardino could not have been painted before his

* All dimensions are given in centimeters.

canonization in 1450. One should accept Longhi's theory that a recorded payment made to Piero's brother Marco in 1462 was connected with this work. The altarpiece is generally considered to have been Piero's first important work, but for the reasons given above, its various parts should be considered separately within a cycle of fifteen years. Longhi notes that Masaccio's influence is still fairly obvious at the start in the figures of *St Sebastian* and *St John the Baptist*. I would also attribute to the initial period *The Crucifixion*, for it reveals a psychological intensity and a dramatic gesticulation far removed from the impassive *Madonna* in

the center. Focillon suggests that the donors kneeling at her feet are also derived from Masaccio. In fact, this group and the figures in *The Crucifixion* have certain features in common, as, for instance, the nervously extended hands of the man in the foreground and those of the hooded figure, both very similar to the hands of the distraught Virgin at the foot of the Cross. This manner of painting hands is absent from Piero's later style: he made them softer, with bent or closed fingers. To sum up, certain parts of the altarpiece have a dramatic emphasis with which the artist was to dispense as his manner grew calmer and more contemplative; and these parts clearly reveal how close he was to his Florentine experiences. Yet other parts belong wholly to Piero's traditional world. Especially so is the central figure of the *Madonna*, with the impassive regularity of her features and her majestic outspread cloak framing her tall columnar form. (See also comments on the individual parts.)

Plate 1

MADONNA OF THE MISERICORDIA.

Plate 2

MADONNA OF THE MISERICORDIA, detail. Male donors at left.

Plate 3

MADONNA OF THE MISERICORDIA, detail. Female donors at right.

Plate 4

MADONNA OF THE MISERICORDIA, detail of plate 2.

Plate 5

MADONNA OF THE MISERICORDIA, detail. Madonna's head.

Plate 6

SS SEBASTIAN AND JOHN THE BAPTIST. Lateral panels at left.

Plate 7

SS ANDREW AND BERNARDINO OF SIENA. Lateral panels at right.

Plate 8a

ST FRANCIS. Small lateral panel at left, above St Sebastian.

Plate 8b

ST BENEDICT. Small lateral panel at right, above St Bernardino.

Plate 9a

THE ANGEL OF THE ANNUNCIATION. Small lateral panel at left, above St John the Baptist.

Plate 9b

THE VIRGIN ANNUNCIATE. Small lateral panel at right, above St Andrew.

Plate 10

THE CRUCIFIXION. Panel directly above the *Madonna of the Misericordia*. The plastic gravity of the Christ has led critics to assume that young Piero travelled from Florence to Pisa in order to study Masaccio's polyptych in the Church of the Carmine there. The polyptych was certainly, at that time, unsurpassed. Focillon points out the "dramatic character, the feverish mime of the gestures" in this *Crucifixion*, adding that the Virgin's hands appear as if they were "their own shadows on a wall." P. Toesca goes so far as to say that Masaccio's influence "led the artist to portray in the lateral figures some excited attitudes which were not true to his temperament." Sir Kenneth Clark writes: "before this luminous sky the Virgin and St John are silhouetted with a truth of tone and economy which remind us of certain works by Daumier and Degas."

Plate 11

THE CRUCIFIXION, detail. St. John.

Plate 12

ST JEROME DOING PENANCE. *Panel, 51 × 38. Berlin, Kaiser Friedrich Museum.* When this panel was cleaned some years ago, a signature and a date were revealed: *PETRI DE BURGO OPUS MCCCCL*. The inscription was first made public in 1924 by Bode, and few critics accepted it. Toesca, in fact, rejected it completely. There are undoubtedly many parts painted by Piero's assistants, but one cannot doubt the authorship of the rest of the painting. Longhi has listed the latter thus: "To Piero belongs not only the Saint's beautiful figure—acknowledged by B. Berenson as well—but also the stool upon which rest his precious books, the smooth rock with a niche for the other volumes and the hanging inkwell; at left the sketch of the unfinished lion, and the road, with its lighted pebbles; to the right, beyond the rock, a few distant trees, and on the left, a clearing. This is the first work signed and dated by the master.

Plate 13

ST JEROME WITH DISCIPLE. *Panel, 49 × 42. Venice, Gallerie dell'Accademia.* Nothing is known about this picture before 1850 when it came to the Venice Gallery as part of the Hellman-Renier Bequest. Inscribed on the tree-trunk to the left: *PETRI DE BURGO SANCTI SEPULCRI OPUS*, and under the figure of the disciple: *HIER. AMADI AUG. F.* The panel dates from about 1450 to 1455, as does the London *Baptism* (plate 14): the landscapes of both pictures are somewhat similar, since both portray the artist's home town, seen from slightly different angles. Crowe and Cavalcaselle recall that in 1408 a Venetian called Amadi commissioned some paintings from Nicolo' di Pietro and Gentile da Fabriano but, as they considered the inscription on this panel to be apocryphal, they came to no conclusions. Longhi, who accepts the authenticity of the signature, now believes that Piero had some contacts in Venice and did in fact go there. One notices the psychological approach in the Saint's tension, and in the burning gaze he fixes upon his follower—who is, oddly enough, a much larger man. Though kneeling, and on the same level as Jerome, his head is slightly higher than the Saint's. Jerome is a beautiful figure, brought into relief by touches of white light; his figure recalls the *figurette* of the *Flagellation* at Urbino (plate 28). The shadow under the folded page of the book Jerome holds is pearl-colored, and on the black binding of the closed book at his side one can see metal studs like drops of light which remind one of Vermeer. Salvini thinks it probable that at this time Piero was already susceptible to the influence of Flemish art.

Plate 14

BAPTISM OF CHRIST. *Panel, 166 × 115. London, National Gallery.* There are no documents on this panel, which was painted for the Priory of St John the Baptist in San Sepolchro. Two wings were added to the panel in 1465 by Matteo di Giovanni, a painter from Siena born in San Sepolchro. In 1807 the priory was closed and the panel transferred to the Cathedral. A dealer named Robinson bought it in 1857; later it was acquired by Uzielli who, in 1861, gave it to the National Gallery. The painting is in good condition in spite of a vertical crack through the center.

Longhi and most critics believe this to have been Piero's first work, dating from about 1440 to 1455. In actual fact many similarities have been pointed out between the Angels on the left and figures by Masolino and Domenico Veneziano. Yet in 1905 Mary Logan stated that the panel should be dated about 1465—which seems excessive to say the least.

In parts of this work Piero's art attains a potential perfection which makes it difficult to believe that it was painted before the lateral Saints in the *Misericordia* polyptych. It seems more probable that the work was executed after the Saints, about 1450–5, and a short time before the first of the Arezzo frescos. Toesca writes: "That feeling for open light which Domenico Veneziano had imparted to Piero has here all the individuality which one finds in the Arezzo frescos, and the composition has all the solemn and monumental qualities of those masterpieces." A. Venturi writes, describing the beauty of the panel and the subtlety of its colors, especially those of the Angels' group: "Three splendid and rigid human trunks, three zones of color, blue the first, white and purple and the other two, delightfully juxtaposed: a blue sleeve brushes against the marble white of a torso, a naked arm in pure alabaster envelops the amethyst-like violet of a robe." (See also plates 15–22.)

Plate 15

BAPTISM OF CHRIST, detail. The Angels.

Plate 16

BAPTISM OF CHRIST, detail. Face of the first Angel on the left.

Plate 17

BAPTISM OF CHRIST, detail. Face of the Angel in the center.

Plate 18

BAPTISM OF CHRIST, detail. Landscape on the right.

Plate 19

BAPTISM OF CHRIST, detail. Christ (upper part of figure).

Plate 20

BAPTISM OF CHRIST, detail. Christ (lower part of figure).

Plate 21

BAPTISM OF CHRIST, detail. Man undressing on the right.

Plate 22

BAPTISM OF CHRIST, detail. The Holy Ghost in the form of a dove.

Plate 23

SIGISMONDO MALATESTA KNEELING BEFORE HIS PATRON SAINT. *Fresco transferred to canvas, 257 × 345. Rimini, Tempio Malatestiano, Chapel of the Relics.* The inscription at the foot of the fresco reads: *SANCTUS SIGISMUNDUS. SIGISMUNDUS PANDULFUS MALATESTA PAN. F. PETRI DE BURGO OPUS MCCCCLI.* Beneath the *œil-de-bœuf* window at right, through which a castle may be seen, the following is written: *CASTELLUM SISMUNDUM ARIMINENSE MCCCCXLVI* (the date the castle, designed by Malatesta himself, was built). The fresco shows Sigismondo Pandolfo Malatesta (1417–68), a generous patron of the temple, kneeling before his Patron Saint, Sigismund. The color of the painting has for the most part, crumbled away; only the hands, the faces and the two hounds, executed with a better fresco technique, survive. The background was originally conceived as a "mirror of different marbles", as Longhi has recently observed (after revising a previous impression), so that the Duke's profile in the center should be clearly seen against a dark background. The castle is not, as some have thought, a false relief but is actually intended to be seen through the round window. L. Venturi has rightly

41

remarked that the positions of the Saint and Duke strongly recall those in the *St Jerome with Disciple* of Venice, but here the composition—organized in diagonals and in depth—gives a totally different impression from the Venice panel. Some have noticed the heraldic quality of the fresco which, despite damage, is still very beautiful, and also its apparently secular vein, with the Prince, instead of the Saint, dominating the center of the picture. It is worth recalling, furthermore, that Alberti was in Rimini during that period, reconstructing the Tempio Malatestiano, and that very possibly the two artists met. Sir Kenneth Clark believes: "Piero's work at Rimini turns into a certainty what has hitherto been only a hypothesis, that he was closely acquainted with Leon Battista Alberti." Argan, on the other hand, (*Brunelleschi*, Milan, 1955), compares the marble background of this fresco to the altar by Brunelleschi in the Pazzi Chapel at Florence. (See also plates 24–7.)

Plate 24

SIGISMONDO MALATESTA KNEELING BEFORE HIS PATRON SAINT, detail. St Sigismund upon his throne.

Plate 25

SIGISMONDO MALATESTA KNEELING BEFORE HIS PATRON SAINT, detail. Duke Sigismondo Malatesta kneeling.

Plate 26a

SIGISMONDO MALATESTA KNEELING BEFORE HIS PATRON SAINT, detail of plate 24.

Plate 26b

SIGISMONDO MALATESTA KNEELING BEFORE HIS PATRON SAINT, detail of plate 25.

Plate 27

SIGISMONDO MALATESTA KNEELING BEFORE HIS PATRON SAINT, detail. The two hounds.

Plate 28

FLAGELLATION OF CHRIST. *Poplar-wood panel, 59 × 81·5. Urbino, Galleria Nazionale delle Marche.* No documents concerning this panel are extant. It was formerly in the old sacristy of the Urbino Cathedral. Upon the steps of the throne at left an inscription reads: *OPUS PETRI DE BURGHI SANCTI SEPULCRI*. The picture is in fairly good condition, in spite of some flaking of the paint and of two horizontal cracks at the level of Christ's face and the tyrant's forearm. This small panel is one of Piero's finest masterpieces and may be one of the "small figures" seen by Vasari in Urbino. It has also been the subject of some controversy on both its theme and date of execution. Ancient local tradition would have it that the three men seen at right were Count Oddantonio of Montefeltro, Duke Federico's step-brother—murdered by conspirators in 1444—between his two wicked counselors, Manfredo dei Pio and Tommaso dell' Agnello, whose unpopular decrees were responsible for a revolt and for the Count's assassination. An inscription seen by Passavant along the base of the panel in 1839 which has since faded, stated: *Convenerunt in unum*, a passage from Psalm II, verse 2: *Astiterunt reges terrae et principes convenerunt in unum adversus Dominum et adversus Christum eius.* This refers to the Passion of Christ: "The Kings of the earth came forward and the princes rallied together against the Lord and against his Christ." Sir Kenneth Clark thinks the panel symbolizes the tribulations of the Church (fall of Constantinople in 1453, Council of Mantua, etc.), and that the bearded figure in Oriental attire is inspired by the memory of Emperor Paleologus. Professor Longhi accepts the local tradition and considers the 1444 revolt to "correspond approximately" to the panel's execution. In his view, therefore, the *Flagellation* was painted earlier than the Arezzo frescos, whereas Sir Kenneth agrees with Toesca that the panel was executed between 1455 and 1460. The architecture is beyond all doubt reminiscent of Alberti, who was not active in the first half of the century and whom Piero is believed to have met in Rimini. One might oppose Longhi's theory, recently supported by M. Salmi, with the objection that even if we accept the traditional interpretation, the date of 1444 would only remain a *terminus ante quem non*; with regard to Sir Kenneth Clark's theory one might suggest that some influence by the artist Piero upon the architect Alberti is not altogether an impossibility. It seems fairly evident, on the other hand, that there is a strong connection between this panel and the Arezzo frescos: the architectural structure if reversed, for instance, is the same as that in *Solomon receiving the Queen of Sheba*. Moreover, the maturity of expression, the bold placing of the two scenes on two distant planes, and the exquisite harmony of colors make it almost impossible not to connect this panel with the Arezzo period. Perhaps it was the result of long winter meditations during the pauses in the San Francesco work during 1455–60. It is interesting to observe the changes in public taste when one reflects that in the *Catalogo delle opere d'arte nelle Marche e nell' Umbria* published in 1896 by Cavalcaselle and Morelli, Barroccio's

Martyrdom of St Sebastian was valued at double the price placed on Piero's panel. (See also plates 29–32 and color plate I.)

Plate 29

FLAGELLATION OF CHRIST, detail. The flagellation scene at left.

Plate 30

FLAGELLATION OF CHRIST, detail. The three figures at right.

Plate 31

FLAGELLATION OF CHRIST, detail of plate 30. Head and shoulders of the central figure.

Plate 32

FLAGELLATION OF CHRIST, detail of plate 30. Head and shoulders of figure at left.

Color Plate I

FLAGELLATION OF CHRIST, detail. The flagellation scene at left and architectural motifs.

Plate 33

MADONNA IN CHILDBIRTH. *Detached fresco, 260 × 203*. Monterchi (*Arezzo*), *Chapel of the Cemetery*. The fresco was detached in 1911, and from 1919 to 1925 remained in the Pinacoteca of San Sepolchro; it was then restored to its original location. Pregnant women worship at the picture to this day, so much so that in 1954 the Mayor of Monterchi refused to lend it to an exhibition in Florence in case during its absence something might happen to a woman in labor and the consequent reactions of this. Piero's mother was born in Monterchi. The date of execution has been a matter of scholarly argument, but the fresco is generally believed to have been painted during Piero's stay in Arezzo: according to Longhi between approximately 1450 and 1455; to Sir Kenneth Clark just after 1460; Focillon favors an earlier period. Sir Kenneth Clark thinks it possible that the artist may have been assisted by others in painting this fresco, and B. Berenson went so far as to exclude it from his initial listing of Piero della Francesca's works. The theme of the pregnant Virgin was almost unknown to Italian art but fairly common, as Sir Kenneth Clark points out, to the iconography of Spain, Flanders, and South Germany. Piero here gave the theme a unique dignity and sense of pride, even of disdain. The Virgin stands motionless between two identical Angels drawn from the same cartoon reversed. Sir Kenneth Clark notes that this Virgin is even more Oriental in its outlines than the *Madonna of the Misericordia*, and that in its calm detachment it recalls the finest Buddhist sculpture.

THE FRESCOS IN SAN FRANCESCO AT AREZZO

(Plates 34–118 and color plates II and III)

Piero painted these frescos on the walls of the choir, a Gothic, square-based structure. The size of the larger scenes is about 11 × 24 feet. In 1447, the wealthy Bacci family of Arezzo, who had been saving money since 1427 for this purpose, commissioned the choir's decoration from the Florentine artist, Bicci di Lorenzo, who died in 1452 when he had almost finished painting the vaulting and the choir arch. It is reasonable to assume that Piero was called to take over immediately, as shown by the close resemblance of his first decorations —two heads of Angels on the vault and two Prophets completed in the niches of the archivolt—to the style of his Rimini fresco of 1451. A document dated December 20, 1466, found in Arezzo, mentions the finished work: the execution therefore took place between 1452 and 1466.

The theme developed by Piero is based upon the story of the True Cross, as told in the *Golden Legend*. The story was greatly venerated in the Middle Ages, and had also been depicted by Agnolo Gaddi in the choir of Santa Croce, Florence, at the end of the fourteenth century, and by Cenni di Francesco in San Francesco, Volterra (1410). Sir Kenneth Clark is inclined to believe that the return to this theme in Piero della Francesca's time was related to the success of the infidels in the Holy Land and could possibly have been a form of propaganda for a new Crusade.

Piero divided the high walls traditionally, into three long horizontal scenes, one above the other, all observed from a normal viewpoint—that is, without the attention to perspective Mantegna had given to his decorations in the Ovetari Chapel in 1448. Della Francesca painted the East and West wall with deliberate and lucid symmetry: the two lower scenes depict two Battles, each taking up the whole length of one wall. Upon each middle section he painted two scenes, side by side, but both observed from the same viewpoint. There is also a correspondence of intentions between the two lunettes, showing respectively the *Death of Adam* and the *Exaltation of the Cross*. On the window wall on either side of the great window are two scenes one above the other, at the level of the two sections on the walls. Two Prophets are depicted at lunette level on the upper parts. (See plan on page 47.)

As shown by the dates, this work made slow progress, and I gladly accept Sir Kenneth Clark's theory that the West wall, which stands alone and is cooler in its tones, and was painted almost entirely by Piero, was decorated first, before the master's visit to Rome in 1459. I also believe—with Sir Kenneth —that the work was later resumed with many more interruptions, and with considerable assistance, upon the East wall, where the colors are warmer and less luminous. Everything leads us to believe that this was the manner in which the work proceeded: the then current practice of painting one horizontal section of the whole choir after another was not followed.

The frescos have suffered. The walls for a long time had to be secured with metal girders, and the cracks which inevitably resulted caused the plaster to crumble in many places. Some scenes were seriously mutilated. Copies made in the nineteenth century by the German artist, A. Ramboux (1790–1866) (in the Düsseldorf Academy), and by the French artist, Loyeux, about 1880 (seen by Longhi in the École des Beaux-Arts, Paris), give us some idea of what the whole composition must originally have looked like. The work was restored in 1860 by Gaetano Bianchi, and more recently by Professor Domenico Fiscali who earned Longhi's praise: Longhi wrote "the frescos have been definitely strengthened." Sir Kenneth Clark, on the other hand, states that he has observed a progressive deterioration of the priceless frescos in the course of the last twenty-five years and thinks it doubtful "how much recent restoration has helped matters." Perhaps the decay is due to the dust which rises continually from the chapel's floor.

This work should be considered Piero's masterpiece. In describing the individual frescos I have thought it advisable to follow the narrative rather than the order of the pictures on the walls or the order in which they were painted.

Plate 34

DEATH OF ADAM. *Fresco, 390 × 747.* General view. The *Golden Legend* tells that when Adam became ill his son Seth went to the gates of Earthly Paradise to ask for oil of mercy with which to cure his father. The Archangel Michael refused him the oil, but gave him instead "a branch of the tree that Adam ate of", and added that "when that bore fruit he should be cured and made whole." When Seth came back he found his father dead and planted this tree upon his grave; "and it endured there unto the time of Solomon." At right of the fresco, Adam, who is aware of his approaching death, has summoned his family. They are four: an old and a young couple, who are now standing around him. This is one of Piero's most remarkable inventions. L. Venturi writes: "The rhythm of the picture goes beyond a simple vision of pause and motion, and creates anew that supreme and solemn moment of the wait for death with an internal tension which never has recourse to dramatic means of expression." On the left, barely visible, Seth is talking to the Archangel. The center, under the great tree—undoubtedly the one Seth planted on his father's grave—depicts the lamentation for the death of Adam; this is a solemn group as they gaze at the dead body of Adam. Particularly noteworthy is the dramatic gesture of the woman raising her arms in grief, a figure so foreign to Piero's calm, contemplative humanity. Sir Kenneth Clark clearly exemplified the modern trend of linking these figures and Greek art in his comparison of the striding man on the left with Hercules cleansing the Augean stables depicted on a metope at Olympia. Longhi, too, mentions an indisputable affinity between the nude young man in the right-hand group and an Apollo Omphalos sculpted some two thousand years earlier. This fresco is entirely the work of Piero, although Sir Kenneth Clark believes that an assistant may have had something to do with the two figures on the left of the picture. A large area of plaster has crumbled, mutilating the tree and part of the scene on the left; and many cracks have appeared in the wall.

Plate 35

DEATH OF ADAM, detail of group on the right. Adam announces his approaching death to his relatives.

Plate 36

DEATH OF ADAM, detail of group on the left. Seth speaking to the Archangel and weeping figures.

Plate 37

DEATH OF ADAM, detail. Figures mourning over Adam's dead body.

Plate 38

DEATH OF ADAM, detail. Seth speaking to the Archangel.

Plate 39

DEATH OF ADAM, detail. Nude young man on the right.

Plate 40

DEATH OF ADAM, detail. Two mourners in the central group.

Plate 41

DEATH OF ADAM, detail. Central figure of group on the right.

Plate 42

DEATH OF ADAM, detail. Head of Adam in the group on the right.

Plate 43

DEATH OF ADAM, detail. Head of Eve in the group on the right.

Plate 44

THE QUEEN OF SHEBA AND HER RETINUE and SOLOMON RECEIVING THE QUEEN OF SHEBA. *Fresco, 356 × 747*. General view. The *Golden Legend* tells how Solomon had the tree, grown from Adam's branch, cut down for his palace, and how it could not be made to fit anywhere. The King's men finally lost patience and made it into a bridge over a small lake. The Queen of Sheba, on her visit to Solomon, wanted to cross to the other side of the lake, but when she came to the bridge, she had a vision that the Savior would be crucified on that same piece of wood. She would therefore not walk over it, but knelt in adoration. This episode is shown on the left-hand of the middle section of the West wall: it occupies slightly more than half of this wall. Against a background of hills, and almost bracketed by two trees, we

see, from left to right, the grooms tending the horses, then the ladies-in-waiting, and finally, on the extreme right, the worshipping Queen. The picture on the right shows Solomon receiving the Queen of Sheba against an architectural background of marble and Corinthian pillars, which Vasari described as "divinely measured"; on the left are Solomon's dignitaries, on the right the Queen's ladies. The picture's scheme almost repeats, in an inverted order, that of the *Flagellation* at Urbino; the same could be said of the Queen's retinue in the two contiguous frescos in the Arezzo choir: indeed, two of the figures are so similar that they might have been traced from the same cartoon. One is tempted to believe Vasari's statement that "Piero would fashion earthen models and clothe them in soft materials, with a great number of folds, and these he would portray endlessly." As all men of great imagination, Piero was satisfied with a limited number of poses and actions, and with a restricted catalogue of human types. I also find significant the importance given by the artist to the meeting of Solomon with the Queen of Sheba (an episode which carries no great weight in the *Golden Legend* narrative) for it stressed Piero's interest in majestic and ceremonial events, his love of pageantry, and the studied behavior of courtiers. Commenting upon the second of these two frescos, R. Longhi wonders if the master was not performing here an *exercitium geometriae occultum nescientis se mensurare animi*. I would think that Piero's creations, instead of being the product of inspirational art which proceeds from impulse toward an objective revision of style, followed the inverse process—beginning as an objective cold

proposition and gradually softening and thawing to become a spectacle. Nicco Fasola notes Piero's freedom in dealing with the strict laws of perspective: she remarks that "the very low standpoint—as regards the second fresco—makes the nearest ladies and gentlemen appear paradoxically tall, but the figures themselves, in relation to the hall, enjoy a measure of independence from the structural scheme. This may be seen by comparing the movement of the heads and the capitals. The assembled court obeys freer and different laws because, in this picture, the human interest takes precedence." Piero was helped in the execution of the first fresco, where the grooms on the left betray another hand, possibly that of Giovanni da Piamonte (or Piemonte). The two pictures are in fair condition, with the exception of some gaps on the extreme right, a large crack between the grooms and the kneeling Queen, and a second crack between the Queen and the column.

Plate 45

THE QUEEN OF SHEBA AND HER RETINUE, detail of plate 44.

Plate 46

THE QUEEN OF SHEBA AND HER RETINUE, detail. Grooms on the extreme left.

Plate 47

THE QUEEN OF SHEBA AND HER RETINUE, detail. Queen of Sheba.

Plate 48

THE QUEEN OF SHEBA AND HER RETINUE, detail. Horses on the extreme left.

Color Plate II

TRIUMPH OF CONSTANTINE, detail. River landscape in the center.

Plate 49

THE QUEEN OF SHEBA AND HER RETINUE, detail. Robes of ladies-in-waiting.

Plate 50

THE QUEEN OF SHEBA AND HER RETINUE, detail. Heads of ladies-in-waiting.

Plate 51

THE QUEEN OF SHEBA AND HER RETINUE, detail. Heads of ladies-in-waiting.

Plate 52

THE QUEEN OF SHEBA AND HER RETINUE, detail of plate 51. Head of first lady on the right.

Plate 53

THE QUEEN OF SHEBA AND HER RETINUE, detail of plate 47. Head of Queen of Sheba.

Plate 54

SOLOMON RECEIVING THE QUEEN OF SHEBA, detail of plate 44.

Plate 55

SOLOMON RECEIVING THE QUEEN OF SHEBA, detail of plate 54. Solomon and the Queen.

Plate 56

SOLOMON RECEIVING THE QUEEN OF SHEBA, detail. Solomon's courtiers.

Plate 57

SOLOMON RECEIVING THE QUEEN OF SHEBA, detail. The Queen's ladies-in-waiting.

Plate 58

SOLOMON RECEIVING THE QUEEN OF SHEBA, detail. Head and shoulders of courtier in plate 56.

Plate 59

SOLOMON RECEIVING THE QUEEN OF SHEBA, detail of plate 57. Busts of first two ladies on the left.

Plate 60

SOLOMON RECEIVING THE QUEEN OF SHEBA, detail of plate 56. Heads of first two courtiers on the left.

Plate 61

SOLOMON RECEIVING THE QUEEN OF SHEBA, detail of plate 55. Heads of Solomon and the Queen.

Plate 62

THE BURYING OF THE WOOD. *Fresco, 356 × 190.* General view. The *Golden Legend* goes on to relate how Solomon was told by the Queen of Sheba that a Man would be nailed on the wood of the tree. By His death "the realm of the Jews shall be defaced and cease to exist." Solomon then ordered the tree to be removed and buried "deep in the ground." Piero was clearly helped in the execution of this fresco: Longhi believes the assistant was Giovanni da Piamonte, because the curly heads of the three figures remind him of an altarpiece in Citta' di Castello signed by that artist in 1456—the date coincides with the painting of the Arezzo frescos. Focillon finds the iconographic invention astounding, and notes that Piero had a passionate interest in concrete objects and in their very substance; the grain of the wood leads him to call the artist: "the painter of reality." Note how the pattern of grain in the Cross matches the ragged clouds in the sky. This scene, based with great daring on a display of crossed diagonals, seems almost a pre-figuration of the *Exaltation of the Cross* (plate 106).

Plate 63

THE BURYING OF THE WOOD, detail. Man carrying the Wood.

Plate 64

THE ANNUNCIATION. *Fresco, 329 × 193.* General view. Longhi believes that this scene is perhaps intended to symbolize the Passion of Christ, episodes from which would have been out of place in this "chivalric recital" (Sir Kenneth Clark). Sir Kenneth thinks, in fact, that the scenes of the Passion "are purposely omitted from the series." One might counter these observations, however, by saying that these events are not dealt with, in any case, in the *Golden Legend*. The scene is symmetrical to the one on the East side of the chapel's window, depicting the *Dream of Constantine* (plate 70): two angelic visitations, one in the dark of a night suddenly illuminated by the Divine Messenger, and the other steeped in daylight—Piero's normal method. The architecture has sometimes been compared with that of the Ducal Palace at Urbino. The figures have such a haughty, aristocratic appearance that a number of critics have believed this picture to constitute an Angel telling St Helena of her mission to discover the True Cross, but the iconography appears beyond all doubt to be that of the Annunciation. The fresco is by Piero alone and is in good condition. This was probably one of the last scenes of the cycle. Sir Kenneth Clark believes it to be the very last, executed about 1466.

Plate 65

THE ANNUNCIATION, detail. God the Father.

Plate 66

THE ANNUNCIATION, detail. Archangel Gabriel.

Plate 67

THE ANNUNCIATION, detail. The Virgin.

Plate 68

THE ANNUNCIATION, detail. The window in the top right-hand corner.

Plate 69

THE ANNUNCIATION, detail of plate 67. The Virgin.

Plate 70

DREAM OF CONSTANTINE. *Fresco, 329 × 190.* General view. The *Golden Legend* explains that "innumerable barbarians" were massed along the Danube, their plan being to overrun and subjugate all the provinces. Constantine assembled his army and set out to battle, but "as soon as he began to pass the river he was much afeared, because he should in the morn have battle. And in the night, as he slept in his bed, an angel awoke him and showed to him the sign of the Cross in Heaven. And on it was written in golden letters: 'In this sign shalt thou conquer'." Against the dark sky we can vaguely distinguish the silhouettes of other tents behind that in which sleeps the Emperor, as the Angel arrives. This is the first great *nocturne* in Italian art. The composition is conceived in terms of depth: from the two soldiers who stand on guard outside —one facing, the other turning his back on the spectator, a formula much used by Piero—to the lieutenant sitting at the foot of the bed, to the Emperor who is lying under his white sheet and red blanket, and finally to the smooth verticality of the tent pole. The parted curtains of the tent remind one, with more formal severity, of the *Madonna in Childbirth* at Monterchi. The lighting of the scene reminds Sir Kenneth Clark of the miniatures in King René's *Livre de Cœur d'Amour espris*, whose date, 1457, coincides with Piero's work. The fresco is damaged in its lower area and the Angel's figure is in very bad condition.

Plate 71

DREAM OF CONSTANTINE, detail. Soldier on the left and lieutenant.

Plate 72

DREAM OF CONSTANTINE, detail. The Angel.

Plate 73

DREAM OF CONSTANTINE, detail. Head of sleeping Emperor.

Plate 74

TRIUMPH OF CONSTANTINE. *Fresco, 329 × 764.* General view. "Then Constantine," the *Golden Legend* proceeds, "felt cheered and assured of victory. He repeated on his forehead the sign of the Cross that he had seen in the sky, ordered his banner to be changed into that sign, and took a golden Cross into his right hand. Then he prayed to God that his right hand, which was holding the Cross, should not become stained with Roman blood and that he might defeat the tyrant without bloodshed." Maxentius fell into the trap and "sank into the deep river." The fresco, in which Sir

Kenneth Clark has seen "the most perfect morning light in all Renaissance painting", is so resplendent with color and rhythm that one hardly perceives the cracks in the wall. The movement of the lances and of the banners compensates the eye in full for the deplorable damage sustained by the painting. A supreme masterpiece, the fresco was most probably executed entirely by the artist. The scheme is neatly cut in two by a stretch of landscape in the center. On the left, the rearing white steed excepted, the victorious army proceeds under the yellow banner and against a pattern of poles and lances rising against the ragged March clouds, white against the blue sky. On the right, the disorderly forest of poles and spears gives a perfect picture of Maxentius' rout. This part of the picture is badly damaged, but a general idea of the whole composition can be obtained from a water-color copy, now in the Düsseldorf Academy which was painted in 1840 by the German artist, A. Ramboux. Sir Kenneth Clark suggests that Piero's insistence here upon Oriental costumes and the solemn parade-ground procession of Constantine's army may have been due to the impression made upon the artist by the splendors of the Council of Florence in 1439; certainly Constantine's features recall those of John Paleologus from Pisanello's medal of that date. As I have said, this is perhaps the only part of the series in which there is no evidence of collaboration. Unfortunately it is also one of the most badly damaged.

Plate 75

TRIUMPH OF CONSTANTINE, detail. Group of horsemen led by Constantine.

Plate 76

TRIUMPH OF CONSTANTINE, detail. Central group.

Plate 77

TRIUMPH OF CONSTANTINE, detail. Profile of Constantine.

Plate 78

TRIUMPH OF CONSTANTINE, detail. Horseman on white steed on the left.

Plate 79

TRIUMPH OF CONSTANTINE, detail. Maxentius sinking in the river.

Plate 80

TRIUMPH OF CONSTANTINE, detail of plate 78. Head and shoulders of horseman.

Plate 81

TRIUMPH OF CONSTANTINE, detail. The bugler on the extreme left.

Plate 82

TRIUMPH OF CONSTANTINE, detail. Banners and masts of Maxentius' army, on the right.

Plate 83

TORTURE OF THE JEW. *Fresco, 356 × 193.* General view. The *Golden Legend* tells how the Empress Helena summoned the Jews to find out from them where Christ had been crucified. She was told of one Judas, the only one to know of the whereabouts of the Cross. This he denied, whereupon the Empress had him placed in a dry well and starved. On the seventh day without food, he asked to be released, promising to reveal the secret. The fresco depicts him being hauled out of the well. The scheme, centered around a pyramid of beams, is beautiful even though

the execution is poor. As in the case of the *Burying of the Wood*, too many assistants contributed to it. Giovanni da Piamonte's hand is fairly clearly seen, especially in the men's curly hair.

Plate 84

TORTURE OF THE JEW, detail. The jailers at left.

Plate 85

TORTURE OF THE JEW, detail. Judas and officer.

Plate 86

THE DISCOVERY AND PROOF OF THE CROSS. *Fresco, 356 × 747.* General view. The Jew led the Empress to a spot where, as the *Golden Legend* tells us, "the earth moved and a fume of great sweetness was felt." (The effect was such that the Jew was converted.) Then Judas dug twenty paces deep and "three crosses were discovered and shown to the Queen; and because he knew not which was the Cross of Our Lord, Judas laid them in the middle of the city and awaited a sign from God; and about the hour of noon there was the corpse of a young man brought to be buried. Judas detained the bier and laid upon it one of the crosses, and after that the second, and when he laid on it the third, anon the body that was dead came again to life." This great fresco is on the East wall, opposite the scenes depicting the Queen of Sheba, with which it shares the aulic atmosphere. On the left the Empress Helena, escorted by her ladies and her dwarf, witnesses the discovery of the three crosses, one of which has already been raised, while a second is being extracted from the ground. Opposite the retinue stand peasants with their spades, perhaps a reminder of the artist's origins—

although Piero, born a country lad, enjoyed the company of courtiers. Vasari was full of praise for the figure of the man leaning upon his spade, and wrote that it "could not be improved upon." The two groups are framed by hills rising on both sides; in the middle background is a walled city with gray and pink houses basking in the sun: a vision that has contemporary enchantment. The parallel furrows in the plowed fields to the right of this picture are checked against the façade of colored marble and Albertian circles on the church which forms part of the adjoining scene, the *Proof of the Cross.* Judas holds the sacred wood above the young man rising slowly from his coffin, his body bathed in sunlight. On the left Helena is kneeling before the cross—her action matches the Queen of Sheba's genuflection on the opposite wall. The ladies around her are also on their knees in a magic circle of suspension and immobility. On the extreme right three strangely hatted Oriental figures gaze in some astonishment at the scene. This is perhaps the best of the East wall frescos, and only Toesca believes he has spotted the hand of an assistant in the group of ladies behind the Empress. The condition is fair, with the exception of damages on the extreme right and some cracks along the cross to the right and on the young man's torso.

Plate 87

THE DISCOVERY AND PROOF OF THE CROSS, detail. The Discovery of the Cross.

Plate 88

THE DISCOVERY OF THE CROSS, detail. One of the workmen.

Plate 89

THE DISCOVERY OF THE CROSS, detail. Landscape.

Plate 90

THE DISCOVERY OF THE CROSS, detail. Workmen.

Plate 91

THE DISCOVERY OF THE CROSS, detail of plate 90. Head of workman.

Plate 92

THE DISCOVERY AND PROOF OF THE CROSS, detail. The Proof of the Cross.

Plate 93

THE PROOF OF THE CROSS, detail. The Empress Helena and her ladies.

Plate 94

THE PROOF OF THE CROSS, detail. Judas raising the Cross over the young man.

Plate 95

THE PROOF OF THE CROSS, detail. The three Orientals on the right.

Plate 96

THE PROOF OF THE CROSS, detail of plate 94. Head of Judas.

Plate 97

THE PROOF OF THE CROSS, detail of plate 93. Head of Empress Helena.

Plate 98

DEFEAT OF CHOSROES. *Fresco, 329 × 747.* General view. The *Golden Legend* relates—not in the the chapter on the Discovery of the Cross, but that on the Exaltation of the Cross—that Chosroes, King of Persia, stole the Cross and had it encased in a strange throne, so that "as he sat upon it, as the Father, he would have on his right the wood of the Cross, in place of the Son, and a cock on his left, in place of the Holy Ghost." Then Emperor Heraclius declared war on Chosroes and defeated his son "on one side of the River Danube." Heraclius urged Chosroes to become a Christian, but "as he would not consent he took out his knife and promptly cut off his head." The fresco depicts the battle being fought with a great display of banners and lances framed by the sky; on the right, near the empty throne of the *Golden Legend*, Heraclius plunges his dagger into the throat of Chosroes' son while the pagan Emperor, kneeling on the ground, meekly awaits his fate. Vasari informs us that among these figures and those surrounding them are portrayed many donors, Luigi Bacci, Carlo Bacci and other gentlemen of Arezzo and some well-known men of letters. Vasari made a strange comment on the battle, in which he appears to have noticed everything that is not there: "Fear, animosity, skill, strength and all the other feelings that may be imagined in men who are fighting." Rightly, Focillon remarks: "Chosroes' men move without hurry, as dependable workmen might do—they are conscientiously attending to their craft of killing." Longhi deplores the fact that this ideal work should have been prostituted by Piero's assistants. This is especially true of Lorentino d'Arezzo who, following this collaboration, did a considerable amount of independent work in which he translated Della Francesca's majestic language into mundane terms. All of this section gives one an impression of dullness and has little in common with the sublime contemplative tranquility of the other frescos. Sir Kenneth Clark, quoting A. Warburg,

agrees that the rider of the white horse (in the foreground, at left of the throne) is undoubtedly derived from a relief on the Arch of Constantine in Rome: this would confirm that the fresco was painted after Piero's visit to Rome in 1459.

Plate 99

DEFEAT OF CHOSROES, detail. Fighting men (left foreground).

Plate 100

DEFEAT OF CHOSROES, detail. Warriors and horses (center group).

Plate 101

DEFEAT OF CHOSROES, detail. Heraclius slaying the son of Chosroes (right).

Plate 102

DEFEAT OF CHOSROES, detail. Fighting men (left of center).

Plate 103

DEFEAT OF CHOSROES, detail. Horseman on the white steed (right foreground).

Plate 104

DEFEAT OF CHOSROES, detail. An "Oriental" trumpeter on the left.

Plate 105

DEFEAT OF CHOSROES, detail. Chosroes (extreme right).

Plate 106

EXALTATION OF THE CROSS. *Fresco, 390 × 747.* General view. The *Golden Legend* tells how Heraclius, having beaten Chosroes, took the Cross back to Jerusalem but as he was about to enter the city, "the stones of the gate came down, and formed a wall." Then an angel told him that Christ himself had entered Jerusalem riding an ass in all humility. "At this, the Emperor wept, bared his feet and shed his robes; then, clad only in his cloak, he took up the Lord's Cross and humbly carried it to the gate." Immediately the gate was reopened.

The picture is neatly divided into two parts for purposes of symmetry, and the Cross carried by the Emperor forms a *pendant* to the tree growing from Adam's tomb in the opposite lunette. The symbolism is clear: from the sin of Adam to Redemption through Christ: *Et medelam ferret inde, hostis unde laeserat* ("And the remedy was to come from the place where the enemy had wrought harm"). The six noble figures on the left are effectively opposed to the human wall formed by Jerusalem's Elders and dominated by the tall man who is seen removing his colossal head-dress before the Emperor. Pérate is right in saying that the composition "achieves its greatest decorative effect because of extreme simplification which, however, is kept within those limits beyond which it would become poverty." Though mostly the work of Piero's assistants, even they could not diminish the beauty of their master's conception. Two large cracks in the wall have damaged the fresco.

Plate 107

EXALTATION OF THE CROSS, detail. The group on the left.

Plate 108

EXALTATION OF THE CROSS, detail of plate 107. The two first figures on the left.

Plate 109

EXALTATION OF THE CROSS, detail of plate 107. The fourth and fifth figures.

Plate 110

EXALTATION OF THE CROSS, detail of plate 107. The third figure.

Plate 111

EXALTATION OF THE CROSS, detail. The Elders of Jerusalem at right.

Plate 112

EXALTATION OF THE CROSS, detail of plate 111. Four kneeling figures.

Plate 113

EXALTATION OF THE CROSS, detail of plate 111. Standing figure removing headdress.

Plate 114

PROPHET. *Fresco, 193 at the base.* This figure and the following one (plate 115) are placed at the top of the window wall, to the left and the right of the window. They have not been identified, but are generally believed to represent two prophets connected with the Passion of Christ. The Prophet on the right (plate 115) is easily one of Piero's most sublime creations—calm, grave, and reflecting formidable moral strength. The comparison with the Prophet on the left (this plate) is so unfavorable that it seems very unlikely that Piero painted both. The Prophet on the left suggests the heavy-handed work of Giovanni da Piamonte.

Plate 115

PROPHET. *Fresco, 190 at the base.* (See comment on plate 114.)

Plate 116

ST AUGUSTINE. *Fresco, 71 at the base.* This figure and that of *St Ambrose* (not reproduced here) complete the series, the "Doctors of the

Church" on the entrance arch, begun by Bicci di Lorenzo in the San Francesco Choir. (See general comment on page 44.)

Plate 117a

HEAD OF ANGEL. *Fresco*. This fresco and the following one (plate 117b) are situated on the south-east part of the choir's vaulting. The two heads and the two Doctors (plate 116) represent the sum of Bicci's work on the vaulting.

Plate 117b

HEAD OF ANGEL. *Fresco*. (See comment on plate 117a.)

Plate 117c

HEAD AND SHOULDERS OF ANGEL. *Fresco, 71 at the base*. This fragment and the following one of *St Peter Martyr* (plate 118) are symmetrically placed on the choir's archivolt. The fragment appears to be Piero's work.

Plate 118

ST PETER MARTYR. *Fresco, 71 at the base*. (See comment on plate 117c.)

Plate 119

ST LUKE THE EVANGELIST. *Fresco. Rome, Basilica of Santa Maria Maggiore*. Professor Longhi, who was the first to attribute this fresco to Piero, describes it: "the only decipherable remainder of the frescos in the ex-Chapel of SS Michael and Peter *ad vincula* in Santa Maria Maggiore." The attribution is generally accepted, and so is its date of execution, 1459, because of the document which proves that Della Francesca was in Rome at that time. Sir Kenneth Clark, who sees a connection between the Evangelist's head and some of Piero's later frescos at Arezzo (notably the officer in the *Torture of the Jew*) considers that the picture's "coarseness of type and facture" suggests the work of a pupil. He does allow, however, that Piero may have painted it.

Plate 120

ST MARY MAGDALEN. *Fresco, 190 × 80. Arezzo, Duomo*. Mentioned by Vasari as being situated "in the Bishopric . . . beside the door of the sacristy", this painting is universally considered an autographed work dating from about the end of Piero's stay in Arezzo. Sir Kenneth Clark notes that the figure's draperies, recalling Masaccio and Donatello, are the most "sculptural" in all of Piero's works. Professor Longhi observes that the figure's head, because of its tonality, must have been "directly modeled." (See also plate 121.)

Plate 121

ST MARY MAGDALEN, detail of plate 120.

Plate 122

RESURRECTION. *Fresco, 225 × 200. San Sepolchro, Pinacoteca Comunale*. This fresco was apparently moved from its original site in the same building, and placed in its present location while Piero was still alive. A document dated 1480 records a sum of money spent on its restoration. Moreover, the architectural style of the building that now houses the painting seems to coincide with that date. Of the Corinthian columns which once framed the picture, only the inner edges are original; the rest is crude restoration. In the eighteenth century the fresco was apparently whitewashed. Sir Kenneth Clark and

Professor Longhi agree in establishing the date of the execution at about the end of Piero's work in Arezzo (1463). Sir Kenneth finds Roman suggestions in Christ's body and in the soldiers, and generally acknowledges in this work a blend of two fundamental aspects of Della Francesca: his taste for courtly refinement and his peasant origins. The same observation comes from Longhi who, writing about the colors, says: "One is at a loss to establish whether or not culture prevails over popular taste." Vasari praised it highly, stating that of all Piero's works in Arezzo, "this is considered the best." The unforgettable figure of the Risen Christ has challenged all critics to recreate it verbally. To quote here, among the many, Sir Kenneth Clark's description: "This country god, who rises in the gray light while humanity is still asleep, has been worshiped ever since man first knew that seed is not dead in the winter earth, but will force its way upwards through an iron crust. Later, He will become a God of rejoicing, but His first emergence is painful and involuntary. He seems to be a part of the dream which lies so heavily on the sleeping soldiers; and has Himself the doomed and distant gaze of a somnambulist." But the Risen Christ does not belong to this world; His naked body and head are not conceived from such a low viewpoint. In drawing the figure of Christ, Piero hesitated perhaps between the magnetism of His head and gaze, and the strong wilful action of the foot pushing His whole body out from the grave. (See also plates 123–5.)

Plate 123

RESURRECTION, detail. Face of Christ.

Plate 124

RESURRECTION, detail. Sleeping soldier on the left.

Plate 125

RESURRECTION, detail. Sleeping soldier on the right.

Plate 126

HERCULES. *Detached fresco, 151 × 126. Boston, Massachusetts, Isabella Stewart Gardner Museum.* The fresco was said to have been painted for the Casa Graziani in San Sepolchro (which might have been Piero's own home). It was uncovered in approximately 1860 by Senator Collacchioni, who moved it to his villa; the painting was returned to Casa Graziani in 1895, sold to a man called Volpi in 1903 and to Mrs Gardner in 1906. The work is generally believed to have formed part of a series of portraits of illustrious men—as was Andrea del Castagno's cycle at Legnaia. Sir Kenneth Clark finds it considerably damaged and restored, and believes the date of the execution to coincide with Piero's last frescos at Arezzo, that is, about 1460–6.

Plate 127

SAINT. *Fresco, 135 × 105. San Sepolchro.* Choir of the former Church of Santa Chiara. This fragment was accidentally discovered on December 23, 1954, in the choir of the church, formerly St Augustine and rechristened Santa Chiara (St Claire) by the nuns of that Order who acquired it in 1555. The building now belongs to the San Sepolchro Philharmonic Society. The fragment must have been part of a mural cycle of which no trace can be found. Salmi believes the figure may be St Julian, but too much is missing for a

57

precise identification. The style entirely agrees with that of Piero in about 1460–5; the handsome fair head, the wonder and seriousness of the eyes, the fleshy mouth recall the Angels in the London *Baptism*; the framing and the marble background are reminiscent of the Rimini fresco of *Sigismondo Malatesta kneeling before his Patron Saint* (plate 23).

THE SAINT AUGUSTINE POLYPTYCH

(Plates 128a–132d)

The documents published by Milanesi in 1885 state that on October 4, 1454, Piero received a commission for a polyptych (*tabulam que est de tabulis compositam*) from Angiolo Giovanni Simone Angeli, for the high altar of the Church of St Augustine in San Sepolchro. In the wording of the contract, the artist was to produce: *tabulam ecclesie et altaris maioris ecclesie . . . ad pingendum et ornandum et deaurandum cum . . . vmaginibus, figuris picturis et ornamentis*. This payment took place on November 14, 1469. Vasari mentions this work: "In the convent of the friars of St Augustine he painted a panel for the main altar, which was a thing much praised." When the church became the property of the Order of St Claire in 1555, the polyptych was removed and taken apart, its place being taken by an *Assumption* of the Umbrian School. In *Art Bulletin* (1941), Millard Meiss put forward a proposal for reassembling the altarpiece and because of his initiative four of the chief panels were tracked down: *St Michael*, in the National Gallery, London (see also the comments on the individual plates); an unidentified Saint—perhaps St John the Evangelist—in New York's Frick Collection; *St Nicholas of Tolentino* in Milan's Poldi-Pezzoli Museum; and *St Augustine*, found in 1947 by Sir Kenneth Clark in the Museum of Antique Art in Lisbon. In 1942 Longhi tried to reconstruct the

predella, the center of which was, in his opinion, the Rockefeller *Crucifixion* in New York. The central panel—probably a Madonna enthroned—is still missing, in addition to the four lateral stories of the predella and three smaller images of Saints from the pilasters. (See plan opposite.)

Plate 128a

ST AUGUSTINE. *Arched panel, 133 × 60. Lisbon, Museo Nacional de Arte Antiga.* This was probably the last panel on the left of the polyptych and was bought in 1936 from Count de Burnay. Before Sir Kenneth Clark's discovery in 1947, it was attributed by the Lisbon Museum to Cima da Conegliano. A large part of the panel is by an assistant. Sir Kenneth allots to Piero the general design, the head, the miter, crozier and other details. The scenes on the cope show interesting connections, such as the *Annunciation*, which is similar to the Arezzo fresco on plate 64. Sir Kenneth believes that the assistant who painted these scenes was also responsible for the Rockefeller *Crucifixion* (plate 132d).

Plate 128b

ST MICHAEL. *Panel, 133 × 59·5. London, National Gallery.* Inscribed on the cuirass are the words: B. ANGELUS POTENTIA DEI LUCHA. The panel was in Milan, the property of a man named

Fidanza, from whom it passed to the antique dealer, Eastlake, and eventually to the National Gallery, in 1867. The inscription led Crowe and Cavalcaselle to believe that Luca Signorelli contributed to this work. Sir Kenneth Clark considers the writing to be connected with the donor's name, or perhaps with the fact that under the high altar on which the picture stood the Blessed Angelo Scarpetti was buried. He, too, has detected the work of an assistant. The face is not well preserved, and the bottom right-hand corner was repainted to conceal the steps of the Madonna's throne in the center. Longhi states that the figure "is charged with parade-ground classicism" and that its effect is made no less disagreeable by the Saint's manner of clasping the dragon's head by its fleshy top.

Color Plate III

THE DISCOVERY OF THE CROSS, detail of plate 88. Workman.

Plate 129a

SAINT. *Panel, 131·5 × 57·8. New York, Frick Collection.* The figure has not been identified with certainty. Meiss believes it to be John the Evangelist because the father and mother of the donor, Angeli, were called Giovanni and Giovanna. The figure is similar to the Saint on the right of the Brera altarpiece (plate 164). Longhi doubtfully suggests St Andrew. From Milan the panel went to the Von Miller Collection in Vienna, and then to its present location. It is believed to be the first figure on the right of the central panel in the St Augustine Polyptych. Longhi thinks that Piero painted this Saint first, and compares it to the figure of God the Father in the Arezzo *Annunciation.* (See also plate 129b.)

Plate 129b

ST NICHOLAS OF TOLENTINO. *Panel, 133 × 60. Milan, Museo Poldi-Pezzoli.* Formerly identified as St Thomas Aquinas until Borenius, in *Burlington Magazine* (1916), explained the significance of the Saint's robe and of the gold star—which shone on Tolentino at the birth of Nicholas. The portrait-like appearance of the picture makes Sir Kenneth

Clark believe that it may depict the donor. The panel is in poor condition, and the hand raised in blessing appears to have been repainted. This should be classed as one of Piero's most monumental masterpieces, because of its solidity and the severe precision of its style.

Plate 130
ST AUGUSTINE, detail of plate 128a. Head of St Augustine.

Plate 131
SAINT, detail of plate 129a. Head of unidentified Saint.

Plate 132a
ST MONICA. *Panel, 39 × 28. New York, Frick Collection.* Formerly in the Liechtenstein Gallery, Vienna. This small panel and the following two (plates 132b and 132c) are believed by Longhi to have been part of the polyptych, and possibly the ones seen by Mancini in 1832 in the choir of the Convent of St Claire —the Order of nuns which took over the Church of St Augustine in 1555. Mancini reported: "a number of small pictures, painted on wood, some of which appear to be in the hand of Piero della Francesca." Sir Kenneth Clark attributes them to an assistant.

Plate 132b
ST APOLLONIA. *Panel, 41 × 28. Washington, National Gallery of Art (Kress Foundation).* Formerly in the Lehmann Collection in New York. (See comment on plate 132a.)

Plate 132c
AUGUSTINIAN SAINT. *Panel, 39 × 28. New York, Frick Collection.* Formerly in Vienna's Liechtenstein Gallery. (See comment on plate 132a.)

Plate 132d
CRUCIFIXION. *Panel, 35·5 × 40·5. New York, John D. Rockefeller Collection.* A. Pope wrote in *Art in America* (1917) that this panel formerly belonged to the Colonna family of Rome. In the first edition of his book, *Piero della Francesca* (1927), Longhi was hesitant about the authorship, but by the second edition (1942) he had no doubts in attributing the panel to Piero. He stated, furthermore, that the execution was originally "all his own work" and that any deterioration in quality was due to restorations carried out years before (1910–15) when the picture was circulated in the Florentine market. Sir Kenneth Clark believes that the panel is by the same assistant who painted the *St Augustine* in Lisbon.

THE PERUGIA POLYPTYCH

(Plates 133–41)
The polyptych(*panel, dimensions of the whole, 338 × 230*) is kept in the Galleria Nazionale dell' Umbria at Perugia and it is composed as follows: in the center the *Madonna and Child enthroned*; on the left *SS Anthony of Padua and John the Baptist*; on the right *SS Francis and Elizabeth of Hungary*; the upper panel shows the *Annunciation* in two roundels in the predella are *St Clare* and *St Agatha* which are just above the three smaller sections with *St Anthony performing a miracle*, the *Stigmatization of St Francis* and *St Elizabeth performing a miracle*. Vasari gives us an accurate description of the altarpiece which he saw in the Convent of Sant' Antonio delle

Monache in Perugia. From there, in 1810, the polyptych was moved to its present location. Vasari appears to have seen on the predella the three sections which are visible now, but it is reasonable to assume that there must have been originally a fourth episode connected with the life of St John the Baptist. The original position of the two roundels —assuming that they were once part of this complex—is not very clear. It is possible, though, that they were part of a base above the predella (see the plan following and the dimensions of the single panels in the comments on the corresponding plates). The obvious diversity of representational language—between the top section that is all perspective, and the middle figures set against a golden background has raised endless doubts about the organic unity of this work. In 1898 Witting stated that the *Annunciation* was a separate entity painted at a later date. This theory, generally rejected at the time, was confirmed after recent restoration (in 1952). The restoration was the subject of an extensive report by Cesare Brandi (*Bollettino d'Arte*, 1954). The upper section, Brandi maintained, had been found narrower than the central part, to which it was very crudely adapted. On the other hand, the unusual shape of the gable would suggest it was original. The radical difference in style between the top and middle sections emphasized by Brandi, would support Witting's theory which I think should be accepted. The recent restoration also clarified some other controversial theories about authenticity: Brandi, for example, points to the gold brocade of the Virgin's robe which, though certainly the work of Piero in the part near the neckline, is elsewhere much coarser in execution. Sir

Kenneth Clark, who attributes some of the figures of Saints to the assistants responsible for the St Augustine, is sure of Piero's execution only in so far as St Elizabeth is concerned. He suggests a later date than that accepted for the altarpiece—completed, as we have seen, in 1469—because of the Child's resemblance to the Jesus of *The Senigallia Madonna* at Urbino (color plate IV). Professor Longhi also favors a later date, and the work, in his view, was executed after the Arezzo frescos; other critics, including Ragghianti, favor an earlier period. As a result of recent restoration much damage has been repaired, especially in the three predelle, which Crowe and Cavalcaselle described in 1864 as being "so ruined and greatly repainted, that they look more like copies than originals by Piero." This part of the altarpiece is generally accepted as the master's own work (see comment on plate 139), while the two roundels are considered the work of pupils (Sir Kenneth Clark).

Plate 133

MADONNA AND CHILD ENTHRONED. *Arched panel, 141 × 65.*

Plate 134

SS ANTHONY OF PADUA AND JOHN THE BAPTIST. *Panel, 124 × 62.*

Plate 135

SS FRANCIS AND ELIZABETH. *Panel, 124 × 64.*

Plate 136

ANNUNCIATION. *Panel, 122 × 194.*

Plate 137a

ANNUNCIATION, detail. The Archangel Gabriel.

Plate 137b

ANNUNCIATION, detail. Virgin.

Plate 138a

ST CLARE. *Panel, measurements of the original part, 21 × 38.*

Plate 138b

ST AGATHA. *Panel, measurements of the original part, 21 × 39.*

Plate 139

STIGMATIZATION OF ST FRANCIS. *Panel, 36·5 × 51·5.* This small panel and the following two (plates 140 and 141) are probably the best part of the Perugia polyptych· The altarpiece is somewhat difficult to analyze in its entirety, and lacks, as we have noted, organic unity; this was due, among other things, to the many different assistants who contributed to its painting. In the *Stigmatization*, as in the *Dream of Constantine*, Piero created a stupendous *nocturne*: his landscape is, as it were, suddenly illuminated by Christ and the solid figures of the two monks do not seem to intrude in the least. The two remaining episodes have been conceived in a rather popular vein. Here the artist reveals the charmingly rural qualities of his background.

Plate 140

ST ANTHONY PERFORMING A MIRACLE. *Panel, 36·5 × 49.* In the bare room, decorated only with the simple geometrical lines of the door, the cradle, and the shelves, the figures acquire a solid bulkiness; the cradle is as peasant-like as the bier of the resurrected young man at Arezzo (plate 92), and the gestures are wisely scanned. Note the curve of the Saint's arm that echoes the outline of the cradle. (See also comment on plate 139.)

Plate 141

ST ELIZABETH PERFORMING A MIRACLE. *Panel, 36·5 × 49.* This small picture has particularly benefited from restoration, for it was more severely damaged than the other two. The legs of the man holding an anchor had been painted over. (See also comment on plate 139.)

THE UFFIZI DIPTYCH

(Plates 142–51)

The measurements of each panel are 47 × 33. The diptych is in the Uffizi Gallery at Florence, and each panel is painted on both sides. On the front are the portraits, bust-length and in profile, of Battista Sforza and her husband Federico II of Montefeltro, Duke of Urbino; on the reverse the Duke and Duchess are allegorically seated in triumphal chariots (see comments on plates 148 and 149). The portraits and the allegories on either side appear against similar landscapes. The diptych came from Urbino to its present location with other possessions of the Della Rovere family in 1631. The date of execution is generally supposed to be about 1465, based on a statement made by a Veronese man of letters in Urbino at that time, but Toesca notes that the statement refers to only one portrait: *Imago eiusdem Principis a Petro Burgensi picta alloquitur ipsum Principem.* L. Venturi, on the other hand, believes the double portrait to have been painted after Battista's death in 1472 and this seems to be confirmed in the lines beneath the *Triumph of Battista Sforza* (see comment on plate 149). Venturi describes her face as "the waxen mask of a dead woman." This theory, however, would compel one to alter the date of the Brera altarpiece, in which the Duke (plate 169) appears to have grown considerably older. Longhi remarks that "the horrible frame of a mock-Renaissance style" around the diptych greatly separates the two portraits which would, if brought together, be united by the landscape's continuity. Sir Kenneth Clark observes that the daring conjunction of a portrait head in the foreground with a distant landscape was invented by Jan Van Eyck (in the *Virgin with Chancellor Rolin*), but he also notes that "Piero has given it a different character by uniting it with the profile pose" and not, as the Flemish master's practice was, with the three-quarter-face pose. Piero reverts to pure profile not perhaps, as Sir Kenneth believes, because he was influenced by Pisanello, but to avoid painting the right side of the Duke's face, disfigured in an accident at a tournament which cost him his other eye. Joubert's words come to mind in this context: *Quand mes amis sont borgnes, je les regarde de profil.* The two scenes of the *Triumphs* are also linked by the landscape, which leads one to believe that the original partition was very thin. Sir Kenneth Clark writes that the two allegorical scenes are "the most Mozartian of all Piero's works. ... The painting of every inch is a joy to the eye, and certain passages are painted with a jeweled touch unequalled except, perhaps, by Watteau." Longhi notices that the surface of the whole diptych is covered by a thick yellowish coat, and that the reverse has been repeatedly scratched. Sir Kenneth Clark has also

detected an alteration to the Duke's neck, originally drawn further in, and more articulated.

Plate 142

PORTRAIT OF BATTISTA SFORZA.

Plate 143

PORTRAIT OF FEDERICO OF MONTEFELTRO

Plate 144

PORTRAIT OF BATTISTA SFORZA, detail. Profile of the Duchess's face.

Color Plate IV

THE SENIGALLIA MADONNA. *Walnut panel, 61 × 53.3. Urbino, Galleria Nazionale delle Marche.* The panel shows a Madonna with the Child in the act of blessing. A male and a female Angel stand on either side of the couple. The panel was formerly in the Church of Santa Maria delle Grazie, outside Senigallia. Restoration carried out in 1952 showed the panel less affected by previous restorers than was feared. In *Bollettino d'Arte,* 1954, Brandi points out that apart from stylistic evidence, the choice of a rare wood such as walnut for the panel is indicative of Flemish influence. This is generally considered a late work by Piero. In 1822, Pungileoni believed it a sketch for the Brera altarpiece. In fact both paintings were for some time attributed to Fra Carnevale. The Flemish quality of the panel, datable about 1475, has constantly been stressed by critics. Sir Kenneth Clark has correctly remarked that "gone are the decorative Albertian incrustations" from the picture's "gray" architecture, and he admits that "some spark of interest in painting [on Piero's part] is still alight." Sir Kenneth has also observed that in this panel Piero's style "verges on mannerism", while the proportions of the Virgin's cloak recall certain portraits by Pontormo. (See also plates 153, 154 and 155.)

Plate 145

PORTRAIT OF BATTISTA SFORZA, detail. Landscape.

Plate 146

PORTRAIT OF FEDERICO OF MONTEFELTRO, detail. Landscape.

Plate 147

PORTRAIT OF FEDERICO OF MONTEFELTRO, detail. The Duke's profile.

Plate 148

TRIUMPH OF FEDERICO OF MONTEFELTRO. Crowned by Victory, the Duke sits in his triumphal chariot, drawn by two white horses, an *Amorino* (Cupid) holding the reins. At the front of the chariot are the four Cardinal Virtues. Beneath it, a Sapphic stanza:

Clarus insigni vehitur triumpho
quem parem summis ducibus perhennis
Fama virtutum celebrat decenter
sceptra tenentem.

("The celebrated [Federico] is borne in great triumph, the fame of his everlasting virtues have proclaimed him a worthy holder of his scepter and the equal of the greatest leaders.")

Plate 149

TRIUMPH OF BATTISTA SFORZA. The chariot is drawn by two unicorns and, as with Federico, they are driven by a Cupid; seated at the front are the three Theological Virtues, while other attendant Virtues stand behind Battista. The Sapphic stanza beneath the painting runs:

Que modum rebus tenuit secundis
coniugis magni decorata rerum
laude gestarum volitat per ora
cuncta virorum.

("She who knew how to be moderate in times of good fortune now is upon the lips of all men, and adorned with praise for the glorious deeds of her great husband.")

Plate 150

TRIUMPH OF FEDERICO OF MONTEFELTRO, detail. Center of picture on plate 148.

Plate 151

TRIUMPH OF BATTISTA SFORZA, detail. Center of picture on plate 149.

Plate 152

MADONNA AND CHILD WITH FOUR ANGELS. *Panel, 42 × 21. Williamstown (Massachusetts), Clark Art Institute.* Officially mentioned for the first time by Gnoli (in *Dedalo*, 1930), who dated it about 1470. The panel belonged to an American collector in Paris who had bought it from the antique dealer, Knoedler, and "did not want anyone else to enjoy it." Longhi observes that "this extreme instance of *Pierolatry* should be recorded as an example of the artist's good fortune!" I could add that it has proved impossible while writing this monograph, to obtain from the present owners a direct photograph of the painting so that it might be reproduced with details. For this reason the reproduction used is from the old photograph which appeared in *Dedalo* in 1930. In the second edition of his monograph on Piero (1942), Professor Longhi analyzed this panel in great detail, rejecting the theories of those who doubted its authenticity and proclaiming it one of the artist's masterpieces. In Longhi's opinion Piero painted it in the period between the completion of the Arezzo frescos and the Brera altarpiece—in 1460-5 rather than in 1465-70.

Plate 153

Plate 154

Plate 155

Plate 156

First mentioned by Vasari as belonging to Piero's descendants, it was sold in 1861 by a Florentine called Baldi to a Mr Barker and purchased for the Gallery in 1874 from the Barker Sale. The painting has often been described as "unfinished", but Sir Kenneth Clark makes it clear that it was, in fact, subjected to a drastic restoration. In some parts, as for instance the two figures of shepherds, the restoration went as deep as Piero's original priming and drawing. The Flemish influence behind the painting has been generally observed, and in this connection Sir Kenneth Clark suggests the panel could not have been painted before the probable arrival at Urbino of Justus of Ghent in 1468. He further points out that the Child's features are very similar to Hugo Van der Goes's Portinari altarpiece in the Uffizi Gallery Justus had been apprenticed to Hugo Van der Goes. But the great Portinari altarpiece arrived in Florence in 1475, and therefore the Nativity could not have been painted before that date.

The landscape is once again the San Sepolchro countryside and very similar, though painted in greater detail, to that in the Baptism of Christ (plates 14 and 18). The characters, however, show here an emotion, a moving sentimental participation in the event, foreign to the earlier Piero. L. Venturi notes that even the hut seems to be painted with an eye to history. Sir Kenneth Clark praises the picture's beauty, even though it was executed at a time when Piero's interest in painting was declining. He compares it with The Uffizi dyptych for the silvery quality of its tone. "Not only the angels but the colors," Sir Kenneth writes, "seem to sing." (See also plates 157-61.)

Plate 157

Plate 158

Plate 159

Plate 160

Plate 161

Plate 162

Brera. The enthroned Virgin, with the Child asleep on her knees, is surrounded by four angels and by SS John the Baptist, Bernard of Siena, Jerome (at left), Francis, Peter Martyr, and John the Evangelist (at right); Federico of Montefeltro kneels at her feet. The panel was moved to the Brera Gallery in 1811 from the Church of San Bernardino near Urbino, built between 1483 and 1491, after Federico's death. The fact that St Bernard appears among the Saints is significant, since it indicates a late date of execution, for the Saint was not canonized before 1450. Longhi believes that Piero painted the panel in or about 1475, while Sir Kenneth Clark tends to consider it a commemoration of the birth of Federico's son Guidobaldo in 1472 —which was also the year Duchess Battista died. Sir Kenneth recalls that a note in the records of the Convent of San Bernardino of Urbino states that the altarpiece of the high altar was painted about 1472 by Fra Carnevale "because the Virgin is a portrait of the Duchess Battista Sforza, and the infant is the likeness of the son born to the Duke by the said Duchess." (The note was first quoted by Pungileoni in 1822.) Vasari too attributes the panel to Fra Carnevale whose pictures, he writes, were studied by Bramante as a young man. Certainly the painting's architecture seems to foreshadow Bramante. Duke Federico appears considerably older here than in the Uffizi portrait and his hands suggest the work of another painter, inclined to naturalism; everyone accepts Longhi's theory that they are the work of Pedro Berruguete, a Spanish artist whose presence at Urbino was documented in 1477—a fact that may help in establishing the panel's date. In any case the altarpiece should be considered one of

Piero's last works, and is of a very high order. Its persistent attribution to the almost mythical Fra Carnevale is no less strange than the low opinion in which it is held by Sir Kenneth Clark. He sees it as proof of Piero's "loss of pictorial appetite" towards the end of his creative life. Sir Kenneth admires the architecture in the panel which he thinks may derive from Alberti's *St Andrew* at Mantua; but the figures, in his view, are "stock" and merely "deposited" there, "without the least interest in the interplay of forms or outlines" —less interesting to the artist, in fact, than the ostrich egg suspended above the Virgin's head. This egg has a symbolic meaning: the reader is recommended to study a paper by M. Meiss, "Ovum struthionis, Symbol and Allusion in Piero della Francesca's Montefeltro Altarpiece" in *Actes du XVII Congrès international d'Histoire de l'art,* The Hague, 1955. (See also plates 163–169.)

Plate 163

THE BRERA ALTARPIECE, detail. The Virgin.

Plate 164

THE BRERA ALTARPIECE, detail. Group on the left.

Plate 165

THE BRERA ALTARPIECE, detail. Duke Federico and group on the right.

Plate 166

THE BRERA ALTARPIECE, detail. Heads of two Angels on the left.

Plate 167

THE BRERA ALTARPIECE, detail. Heads of two Angels on the right.

Plate 168

THE BRERA ALTARPIECE, detail of plate 165. Tradition has it that Piero portrayed in the likeness of St Peter Martyr, his pupil and plagiarist, Luca Pacioli.

Plate 169

THE BRERA ALTARPIECE, detail. Profile of Duke Federico.

LOST PAINTINGS

Vasari stated in his *Life of Piero della Francesca, Artist, of Borgo a San Sepolchro*, that the master painted the works that follow, listed alphabetically:

ANCONA

In the Church of San Ciriaco, "for the Altar of St Joseph, the *Marriage of Our Lady*."

AREZZO

In Santa Maria delle Grazie "a *St Donato*, in Bishop's attire and surrounded by children, and a *St Vincent* in a niche in the Church of St Bernard."

FERRARA

"In the Palace he painted many rooms and a Chapel in the Church of St Augustine, decorated with frescos."

LORETO

"Together with Domenico Veneziano he began to paint a work upon the sacristy's vault" (this was later completed by Signorelli).

ROME

In the Vatican "two episodes in the upper rooms" (now known as Heliodorus' Chamber). But in Vasari's *Life of Raphael* only one finished episode is mentioned.

SAN SEPOLCHRO

"In the Parish Church he painted a fresco . . . two saints."

SARGIANO (Province of Arezzo)

"In a chapel a Christ, praying in the garden, at night."

URBINO

"Many beautiful pictures of small figures, most of which have been ruined or lost because of wars that have ravaged that State." Among these pictures, however, might have been the *Flagellation of Christ* and perhaps *St Jerome with Disciple*.

Other documents mention the following works:

AREZZO

A banner with the *Annunciation* on both sides for the Company of the Annunciation (see Biographical Notes, 1466 and 1468).

SAN SEPOLCHRO

Frescos in the Church of the Badia and a fresco of a *Madonna* for the Company of the Misericordia (see Biographical Notes, 1474 and 1478).

PAINTINGS ATTRIBUTED TO PIERO DELLA FRANCESCA

Plates 170–1

MADONNA AND CHILD and, on the reverse, STUDY IN PERSPECTIVE. *Panel, 53 × 41, Florence, Contini-Bonacossi Collection.* This panel is in poor condition; an inscription on it, dated 1655, claims it to be by Leonardo da Vinci. Longhi attributes it to Piero and describes it as "the earliest work by the master to have come into our possession." The work is datable about 1440 and was painted in Florence during the period when Piero was obviously influenced by Domenico Veneziano. This is proved by the softness of the chromatic passages and by the "intense perspective research which at that time had become an obsession in Florence's artistic circles" (Longhi). The same critic, commenting upon the reverse of the panel calls it a "perfect model" for the mosaic woodwork which Cristoforo da Lendinara was to carve some forty years later. The attribution has been accepted by Salmi.

Plates 172–3

ARCHITECTURAL PERSPECTIVE. *Panel, 60 × 200. Urbino, Galleria Nazionale delle Marche.* This splendid work and two others, of lesser quality, in Baltimore and Berlin, are painted with colors characteristic of Piero. Critics are divided in two groups about this panel. Some—from Crowe and Cavalcaselle (1864) to Sir Kenneth Clark (1951)—have no hesitation in attributing it to Piero; many others, from Bianchini (1724) to Brandi (1949) favor Luciano Laurana because of an inscription (now disappeared) which read URANNA. Yet others believe the panel to have been painted by Francesco di Giorgio Martini, or by Baccio Pontelli; Focillon and Toesca believe it the work of Piero's school. Sir Kenneth Clark thinks the panel was originally the front of a chest; Mariani and others believe it to be an early example of a theatrical set. Sir Kenneth examines at some length the possibility of Piero having engaged in architectural activities, and notes that works such as the *Flagellation of Christ* and *The Proof of the Cross* display definite technical knowledge. In his opinion Piero may have advised Federico of Montefeltro in the planning and building of the Urbino Ducal Palace. In attributing this work to Piero, Sir Kenneth sees it as a last tribute by him to Alberti.

Plate 174

SIGISMONDO PANDOLFO MALATESTA. *Panel, 44·5 × 34·5. Florence, Contini-Bonacossi Collection.* Attributed to Piero by Longhi who is certain that it was painted in 1451, because of the panel's similarity—even in measurements—to the Rimini fresco.

Plate 175

ST LUDOVIC. *Detached fresco, 123 × 90. San Sepolchro, Pinacoteca Comunale.* Formerly in the Palazzo Pretorio.

An inscription upon the panel, mentioned by Dragomanni in 1835, stated that it was painted for Ludovico Accaiuoli in 1460. The attribution to Piero is traditional, and Sir Kenneth Clark, for one, is rather inclined to accept it. Most modern critics, however, believe it the work of a bad imitator, perhaps Lorentino.

Plate 176

THE VILLAMARINA MADONNA. *Panel, 63 × 55. Rome, Galleria Nazionale d'Arte Antica (Villamarina Collection).* Attributed to Piero by Lionello and Adolfo Venturi. B. Berenson believes it a work by Signorelli, and other critics believe the painter was a close follower of Della Francesca.

FEMALE PORTRAIT. *Panel, 58 × 38. New York, Lehmann Collection.* An inscription added at a later date states that this is a portrait of the Duchess of Urbino painted by Piero. B. Berenson accepts this with some reservations; others attribute the panel to Paolo Uccello or to Veneziano. Arcangeli considers it "not unworthy" of Piero.

HEAD OF YOUNG WOMAN. *Turin, Gualino Collection.* The attribution to Piero is by B. Berenson.

STORIES FROM THE LIFE OF ST DONATO. *Fragments of frescos. Arezzo, building adjoining Santa Maria delle Grazie.* Attributed to Piero by B. Berenson and Van Marle.

MALE FIGURE (of beholder in the *Crucifixion* by Orcagna). *Fresco. Florence, Convent of Santo Spirito.* This bold and interesting attribution was proposed by C. L. Ragghianti in *Critica d'Arte*, 1954. He believes the figure to have been inserted in 1439, when Piero was working in Florence with Domenico Veneziano.

LOCATION OF PAINTINGS

AREZZO

CHURCH OF ST FRANCIS
Death of Adam (plates 34–43).
The Queen of Sheba and her retinue and *Solomon receiving the Queen of Sheba* (plates 44–61).
The Burying of the Wood (plates 62–3).
The Annunciation (plates 64–9).
The Dream of Constantine (plates 70–3).
Triumph of Constantine (plates 74–82 and color plate II).
Torture of the Jew (plates 83–5).
The Discovery and Proof of the Cross (plates 86–97 and color plate III).
Defeat of Chosroes (plates 98–105).
Exaltation of the Cross (plates 106–13).
Prophets (plates 114–15).
St Augustine (plate 116).
Heads of Angels (plates 117a–b).
Head and Shoulders of Angel (plate 117c).
St Peter Martyr (plate 118).

DUOMO OF AREZZO
St Mary Magdalen (plates 120–1).

BERLIN

KAISER FRIEDRICH MUSEUM
St Jerome doing penance (plate 12).

BOSTON (Massachusetts)

ISABELLA STEWART GARDNER MUSEUM
Hercules (plate 126).

FLORENCE

CONTINI-BONACOSSI COLLECTION
Madonna and Child and *Study in Perspective* (plates 170–1; attributions).
Sigismondo Pandolfo Malatesta (plate 174; attribution).

UFFIZI GALLERY
Diptych (plates 142–51).

LISBON

MUSEU NACIONAL DE ARTE ANTIGA
St Augustine (plates 128a and 130).

LONDON

NATIONAL GALLERY
Baptism of Christ (plates 14–22).
St Michael (plate 128b).
Nativity (plates 156–61).

MILAN

MUSEO POLDI-PEZZOLI
St Nicholas of Tolentino (plate 129b).

PINACOTECA DI BRERA
Altarpiece (plates 162–9).

MONTERCHI (Arezzo)

CHAPEL OF THE CEMETERY
Madonna in Childbirth (plate 33).

NEW YORK

FRICK COLLECTION
Saint (plates 129a and 131).
St Monica (plate 132a).
Augustinian Saint (plate 132c).

JOHN D. ROCKEFELLER COLLECTION
Crucifixion (plate 132d).

PERUGIA

GALLERIA NAZIONALE DELL' UMBRIA
Polyptych (plates 133–41).

RIMINI

TEMPIO MALATESTIANO
Sigismondo Malatesta kneeling before his Patron Saint (plates 23–7).

ROME

BASILICA OF SANTA MARIA MAGGIORE
St Luke the Evangelist (plate 119).

GALLERIA NAZIONALE D'ARTE ANTICA
The Villamarina Madonna (plate 176; attribution).

SAN SEPOLCHRO

PINACOTECA COMUNALE
Misericordia Altarpiece (plates 1–11).
Resurrection (plates 122–5).
St Ludovic (plate 175; attribution).
For the figure of the *Saint* in plate 127 please see comment, page 57.

URBINO

GALLERIA NAZIONALE DELLE MARCHE
Flagellation of Christ (plates 28–32 and color plate I).
The Senigallia Madonna (plates 153–5 and color plate IV).
Architectural Perspective (plates 172–3; attribution).

VENICE

GALLERIE DELL'ACCADEMIA
St Jerome with Disciple (plate 13).

WASHINGTON

NATIONAL GALLERY OF ART
St Apollonia (plate 132b).

WILLIAMSTOWN
(Massachusetts)

CLARK ART INSTITUTE
Madonna and Child with four Angels (plate 152).

SELECTED CRITICISM

The monarch of our times of painting and architecture, Maestro Piero deli Franceschi, made famous, thanks to his brush, at Borgo San Sepolchro and, as one can see, also at Urbino, Bologna, Ferrara, Arimino, Anconna and in our own land, whether in oils or gouache, on murals or woods, but especially in the city of Arezzo, where he painted that great chapel, one of Italy's most worthy achievements and one acclaimed by all; then he wrote the book about perspective which can be found in the magnificent library of our most illustrious Duke of Urbino.

FRA LUCA PACIOLI
De divina proportione (1497), 1509.

Pietro dal Borgo was excellent at perspective which he taught to Bramante, a cosmographer, a popular poet and a good painter.

FRA SABBA DA CASTIGLIONE
Ricordi overo Ammaestramenti, 1549.

There (in the Church of San Francesco at Arezzo) are frescos with many admirable qualities; among others, the new treatment of the draperies worn by the attendants of the Queen of Sheba. This work contains also many portraits from life and a range of Corinthian columns, the proportions of which are divine in their perfection. A peasant leaning upon his spade as he listens to the discourse of St Helena has a concentration so well expressed that it could not be improved. The dead body restored to life at the touch of the Cross, and St Helena's joy, are executed as excellently as the arrangement of the bystanders who prostrate themselves in adoration. But best of all is the treatment of night in the picture of the *Dream of Constantine*. An angel descends, head downward, bearing the insignia of victory to the Emperor asleep in his tent and guarded by armed men seen partially

through the darkness. The light comes from the angel alone. It is very well handled. In this work Piero shows the importance of copying things as they really are. Later artists have been able to profit by his example.   GIORGIO VASARI
Le vite, 1568

There is much that is antique left in his work; the drawing is arid, the folds are too detailed and precious, the feet are well fore-shortened but too far apart from each other. For the rest, in the air and in the coloring of the figures, one can see the beginnings of that style which was later improved by his pupil, Pietro Perugino, and perfected by Raphael.   LUIGI LANZI
Storia pittorica della Italia, 1789.

He was, however, impersonal, not in his method only, as all great artists have to be, but he was what would be commonly called impassive, that is to say, unemotional, in his conceptions as well. He loved impersonality, the absence of expressed emotion, as a quality in things. Having, for artistic reasons, chosen types the most manly, and, for perhaps similar reasons, a landscape which happens to be of the greatest severity and dignity, he combined and recombined them as each subject required, allowing the grand figures, the grand action, and the severe landscape, these, and these alone, to exercise upon us, as they must when all special emotion is disregarded, their utmost power. He never asks what his actors feel. Their emotions are no concern of his. Yet no "Flagellation" is more impressive than one of his, although you will not find on the face of any of the drama-tis personae an expression responsive to the situation; and, as if to make the scene all the more severely impersonal, Piero has introduced into this marvelous picture three majestic forms who stand in the foreground as unconcerned as the everlasting rocks. And so, in his fresco of the "Resurrection", Piero has not even thought of asking himself what type of person Christ was. He chose one of the manliest and most robust, and in the gray watered light of the morning, by the spreading cypresses and plane trees, you see this figure rising out of the tomb. You feel

the solemnity, the importance of the moment, as in perhaps no other version of this subject; and, if you are a person sensitive to art, you will have felt all this before you have thought of asking whether Christ looks appropriately Christ-like, or whether there is a fit expression on His face. BERNARD BERENSON
Italian Painters of the Renaissance, 1897.

When looking at his works, of such an unchangeable and perfect serenity, and exclusively dominated by decorative harmony, one has the impression that Piero had remained, in that second half of the fifteenth century—a period so full of vitality and fashion— the last of the primitives, the heir of Giotto and Angelico; a primitive, though, who does not ignore the discoveries of the new science and who, by applying this science without making an exhibition of it, subordinates everything to the plastic rhythms of lines and colors. ANDRÉ PÉRATÉ
in *Histoire de l'art* by A. Michel, 1908.

With reference to form, perspective induces Piero to organize everything inside the most simple and monumental contours. It is as if everything should really become one of the five regular bodies in order to assist the perspective construction, which is essential construction laid out in planes converging upon an ideal axis; Piero wants us to feel space as a regular volume by inserting into it other regular volumes. . . .

This is why Piero feels the need for a monumental human form, striking a statuesque pose, remaining apart from the others, and portrayed during a suspended gesture. This has been misunderstood by the psychological critics who have imputed these general rules alternatively to lack of feeling, pride, or hieratic heroism; and yet it would be quite easy to explain that it is all inevitably due to perspective vision, which must require a static and well-defined presentation, either entirely solar or entirely artificial—as in the London *Baptism* or in the *Dream of Constantine*—so as to stress in each particular case the form and color.

And here we come to the problem of color which Piero can blend with all his other pictorial results so well, that almost every one of his works, having first given us the impression of an enormous convergence of depths and of forms contained within boundaries of straight lines and a few ample curves, later appears as a gigantic assembly of placid, powerful areas that surface in perspective due to the continuity and order of his masses.   ROBERTO LONGHI
"Piero dei Franceschi e lo sviluppo della pittura veneziana", in *L'Arte*, 1914.

This grave and primitive humanity [of Masaccio] confronted Piero as an unopposable term of priority; without Masaccio, Piero's humanity would have been different, though this does not mean that their two humanities are related. Piero's man was admittedly the same as the one created by Masaccio, but he was no longer left to the hostility of a world which he must perforce dominate by the strength of his own plastic or moral isolation; in fact, as he evolved he came to terms with himself, earth, the costumes, light and colors that he paints. But we should remember that Piero's concept of man does not stem wholly from Masaccio's work, but was also influenced by the works of other artists.   ROBERTO LONGHI
Piero della Francesca, 1927.

Never did we experience a stronger feeling of intellectual certainty than when we contemplated those walls decorated midway through the fifteenth century, in a Tuscan city, by a master from Umbria. After so many studies of Italy, after the successive preferences of various generations for so many different masters, it is perhaps here today that we find ourselves, as never before, in complete agreement with ourselves. All have experienced it, both historians and poets. We are now paying homage once again to the man who, in his time, was rightly described in regal terms as "the monarch of painting", for the peaceful domination that he exercised over the spirits of his fellow men.

What do we see in those frescos? *Lucidus ordo*: a definite order imposed by the light of the spirit, a calculated order of all the parts, in which however, calculation is not an end in itself, but tends towards man as illustrating a world free of all commotion and of all convulsion, a man who is the radiant master of his Garden of Eden. Through the formidable scenes recorded in the most ancient archives of humanity, the impersonal dignity of Piero's figures express a higher and more serene mission than disaster, despair, and death. HENRI FOCILLON

Piero della Francesca (1934-5), 1952.

As a painter, he defined the volumes of bodies, and their relationship to space with such an intensity that he transformed his findings into indisputable revelations; in this he turned to his advantage even the most unstable elements, such as light and color. As a theorist, he imparted to this precision a mathematical rigor. For him color, though diaphanous and brilliant, was a solid tegument of form, and this principle he applied not only to his frescos but also to his panels, where the oils technique—in the use of which he was encouraged by the Flemish masters— helped him to produce a more throbbing effect. He did not co-ordinate light to dramatic action, as Masaccio and Andrea del Castagno had done; he did not see light as fluid outlines, as Filippo Lippi, nor did he employ it to dissolve plastic solidity, as was the practice of Domenico Veneziano. He made of light the dominating element of each and every image, seen for itself as it operates, neither inconstant nor sudden, but endowed with an actual stability that increases its intensity: a solar light, all-devouring; the light of open skies in all its transparency, rendering everything lucid; light that defeats shadows and darkness. And where he passed, the traces of his inimitable art remained and contributed to new studies of light by the artists of Ferrara, of Emilia, and of Latium. PIERO TOESCA

in *Enciclopedia Italiana*, XXVII, 1935.

An entirely different importance should be attributed to the direct relationship between Piero's art and that supreme form of art that was Venetian painting. Once again it was the harmony between form and color, achieved by Piero on the basis of perspective, that was to pave the way for the famous *colorismo* of the Venetians and the spacious epic works of Giovanni Bellini, Antonello da Messina, Carpaccio and, later still, for the young Titian and Veronese.

Later, too, after the long pause described variously as "Baroque" or "Romantic", that age-old search for formal and chromatic measure was to reappear in the art of those who had either participated in, or followed, the lyric poetry of Impressionism: Cézanne, Seurat, and some exponents of "synthetism". Herein lies the unconscious reason for the temporary return to Piero della Francesca, not on the part of the critics—which would be less important—but of the artists themselves.

ROBERTO LONGHI
"Piero in Arezzo", in *Paragone*, 1950.

Although deeply conscious of the prime factors in life and art, he is far from being primitive. He is, in the full, critical sense of the word, a classic artist, and to a large extent his rediscovery was part of a new classicism, of which Cézanne and Seurat were the living manifestations. It is not surprising that the admirers of Cézanne took a different view of Quattrocento art than the admirers of Burne-Jones. They were looking not for phantasy, but for order; not for grace, but for solidity. The word "blocks", applied to Piero's figures as a term of reproach by Crowe and Cavalcaselle, became a term of praise in the new concept of pictorial architecture. In particular Piero's application of geometry, not only to whole compositions but to individual figures, was in harmony with the spirit which was later to find expression in Cubism and its derivatives. This was the period in which our whole notion of "the primitive" was transformed.

SIR KENNETH CLARK
Piero della Francesca, 1951.

If one were to expect one work only to represent the essence of Italian painting, Piero della Francesca's last creation, the Brera altarpiece, should be chosen for its value as an *exemplum*. The deification of man was Humanism's triumph and because of this, Piero's altarpiece is symbolic of the fifteenth century's spiritual civilization. But it also contains a message for the future. The Museum's fixed lighting detracts from some of the variations and vibrations of that enchanting silver light which floods the architecture and lends forms to their perspective; only the observer who has seen Piero's painting in a natural atmosphere can have an idea of the miracle that it is. And yet even the most absentminded visitor can note to what extent Piero had progressed beyond mere Florentine drawing, how his rarefied volumes were achieved due to a condensation, on plastic planes, of the mysteriously colored air pervading the whole work. Such a construction of luminous quantities . . . paves the way to Giovanni Bellini. . . . We are deeply moved by this sublimation of Piero della Francesca's pictorial genius, nourished by the greatest scientific and philosophical knowledge of the Renaissance, asserting the most absolute intellectuality, and which, the evening before its death, sings with pure lyric tones.

FERNANDA WITTGENS
Piero's Urbino Altarpiece, 1952.

Piero's love for Eastern costumes, fantastic arrangements, and chivalric atmosphere could indeed be described as typical of a man of the people. But the very conception behind these representations shows how Piero could introduce in them that corrective element which the populace usually apply to luxury and ostentation: irony. Irony is present, here and there, in the details of the Queen of Sheba's ladies, among the grooms, among the men who are sent to return the Cross (all of these works are part of the Arezzo frescos); this irony is indicative of the artist's detachment from his theme and allies itself admirably to a geometrical abstraction of forms. In fact irony and abstraction are like a screen, however transparent it may be, between the artist and reality. Yet in spite of this Piero could be a realist in his own fashion.
LIONELLO VENTURI
Piero della Francesca, 1954.

80

BIBLIOGRAPHICAL NOTE

An extensive bibliography on Piero della Francesca extending to 1927 can be found in Roberto Longhi's monograph (1927) which was amended but not brought up to date in the second edition of 1942. A good bibliographical note is included in the Catalogue of the "Exhibition of Four Masters of the Early Renaissance" organized in Florence in 1954. Only the most important and most recent works are quoted here.

B. BERENSON. *The Central Italian Painters of the Renaissance*, New York and London, 1897.
A. VENTURI. *Storia dell'arte italiana*, VII, 1; Milan, 1911.
R. LONGHI. "Piero dei Franceschi e lo sviluppo della pittura veneziana", in *L'Arte*, 1914.
G. GRONAU. In *Künstler-Lexikon*, Thieme-Becker, Leipzig, 1916.
A. VENTURI. *Piero della Francesca*, Florence, 1922.
R. LONGHI. *Piero della Francesca*, Rome, 1927; and Milan, 1942 (2nd edition).
R. VAN MARLE. *The Development of the Italian Schools of Painting*, The Hague, 1929.
H. FOCILLON. *Piero della Francesca* (lectures, 1934–5), Paris, 1952.
P. TOESCA. In *Enciclopedia italiana*, XXVII, 1935.
J. VON SCHLOSSER. *Xenia*, Bari, 1938.
C. GILBERT. "New Evidence for the Date of Piero della Francesca's Count and Countess of Urbino", in *Marsyas*, 1941.
M. MEISS. "A documented Altarpiece by Piero della Francesca", in *The Art Bulletin*, 1941.
M. SALMI. "Piero della Francesca e Giuliano Amedei", in *Rivista d'arte*, 1942.
M. SALMI. "La Bibbia di Borso d'Este e Piero della Francesca", in *La rinascita*, 1943.
M. SALMI. *Piero della Francesca e il Palazzo Ducale di Urbino*, Florence, 1945.
M. SALMI. "Un'ipotesi su Piero della Francesca", in *Arti figurative*, 1947.
K. CLARK. "Piero della Francesca's St Augustine Altarpiece", in *The Burlington Magazine*, 1947.
J. ALAZARD. *Piero della Francesca*, Paris, 1948.
B. BERENSON. *Piero della Francesca o dell'arte non eloquente*, Florence, 1950.
R. LONGHI. "Piero in Arezzo", in *Paragone*, 1950.
K. CLARK. *Piero della Francesca*, London, 1951.
R. LONGHI. *Piero della Francesca—La leggenda della Croce*, Milan, 1951.
F. WITTGENS. *La pala urbinate di Piero*. 2 vols., Milan, 1952.
L. VENTURI. "Piero della Francesca, G. Seurat, J. Gris", in *Diogène*, 1953.
L. VENTURI. *Piero della Francesca*, Geneva, 1954.
U. BALDINI. in *Mostra di quattro maestri del primo Rinascimento*, Florence, 1954.

REPRODUCTIONS

ACKNOWLEDGMENT FOR
PLATES

Plates 1 to 5, 8a to 9b, 28 to 39, 41 to 43, 52, 53, 60 to 66, 68, 70, 71, 74, 76, 78, 83 to 85, 88, 90, 91, 93 to 98, 100 to 104, 113 to 115, 121, 172–3 and 176: *Anderson, Rome*. Plates 6, 7, 10 to 13, 122, 123, 129b, 142, 143, 148, 149, 153 to 155 and 175: *Brogi, Florence*. Plates 14 to 22, 128b and 156 to 161: *National Gallery, London*. Plates 23 to 27, 116 to 117c, 127, 133 to 141, 144 to 147, 151: *Gabinetto Fotografico della Sovrintendenza alle Gallerie, Florence*. Plates 40, 44, 45, 54, 67, 69, 72, 73, 75, 77, 79 to 82, 86, 87, 89, 92, 99, 105 to 112, 118, 124 and 125: *Claudio Emmer, Milan*. Plates 46 to 51, 55 to 59, 120, 128a, 130, 170 and 174: *Alinari, Florence*. Plate 119: *Cesare Gerbi, Rome*. Plate 126: *Gardner Museum, Boston*. Plates 129a, 131, 132a and 132c: *Frick Collection, New York*. Plate 132b: *National Gallery of Art, Washington*. Plate 132d: *John D. Rockefeller Collection, New York*. Plate 152: From the magazine *Dedalo*. Plate 171: *Contini-Bonacossi Collection, Florence*. Plates 162 to 169: *Gabinetto Fotografico della Pinacoteca di Brera, Milan*. The four color plates have been selected by *Claudio Emmer, Milan*.

Plate I. MADONNA OF THE MISERICORDIA, San Sepolchro

Plate 2. *Detail of plate 1*

Plate 3. *Detail of plate 1*

Plate 4. *Detail of plate 2*

Plate 5. *Detail of plate 1*

Plate 6. SS SEBASTIAN AND JOHN THE BAPTIST, San Sepolchrò

Plate 7. SS ANDREW AND BERNARDINO OF SIENA, San Sepolchro

Plate 8. ST FRANCIS *and* ST BENEDICT, San Sepolchro

Plate 9. ANNUNCIATION: ANGEL *and* VIRGIN, San Sepolchro

Plate 10. THE CRUCIFIXION, San Sepolchro

Plate 11. *Detail of plate 10*

Plate 12. ST JEROME DOING PENANCE, Berlin

Plate 13. ST JEROME WITH DISCIPLE, Venice

Plate 14. BAPTISM OF CHRIST, London

Plate 15. *Detail of plate 14*

Plate 16. *Detail of plate 15*

Plate 17. *Detail of plate 15*

Plate 18. *Detail of plate 14*

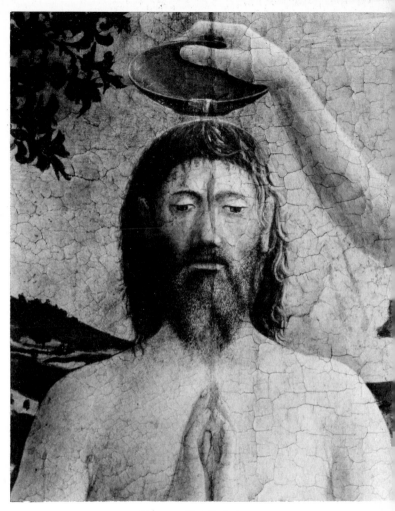

Plate 19. *Detail of plate 14*

Plate 20. *Detail of plate 14*

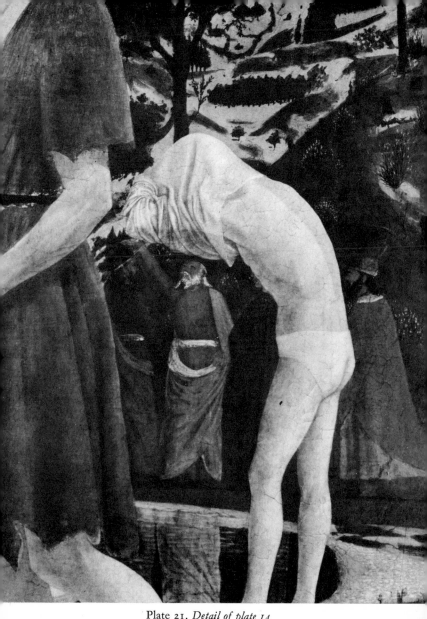

Plate 21. *Detail of plate 14*

Plate 22. *Detail of plate 14*

Plate 23. SIGISMONDO MALATESTA KNEELING BEFORE HIS
PATRON SAINT, Rimini

SANCTVS SIGISMVNDVS · SIG SMVNDVSPANDVLFVS MALATESTA PAN

Plate 24. *Detail of plate 23*

Plate 25. *Detail of plate 23*

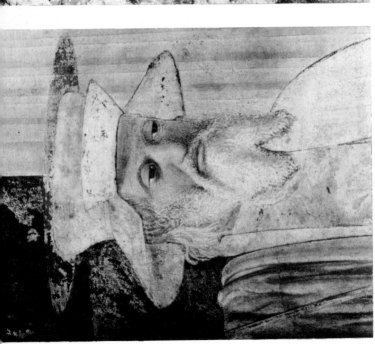

Plate 26. *Details of plates 24 and 25*

Plate 27. *Detail of plate 23*

Plate 28. FLAGELLATION OF CHRIST, Urbino

Plate 29. *Detail of plate 28*

Plate 30. *Detail of plate 28*

Plate 31. *Detail of plate 30*

Plate 32. *Detail of plate 30*

FLAGELLATION OF CHRIST, Urbino (*detail of plate 28*)

Plate 33. MADONNA IN CHILDBIRTH, Monterchi

Plate 34. DEATH OF ADAM, Arezzo

Plate 35. *Detail of plate 34*

Plate 36. *Detail of plate 34*

Plate 37. *Detail of plate 34*

Plate 38. *Detail of plate 36*

Plate 39. *Detail of plate 35*

Plate 40. *Detail of plate 37*

Plate 41. *Detail of plate 35*

Plate 42. *Detail of plate 35*

Plate 43. *Detail of plate 35*

Plate 44. THE QUEEN OF SHEBA AND HER RETINUE AND
SOLOMON RECEIVING THE QUEEN OF SHEBA, *Arezzo*

Plate 45. *Detail of plate 44*

Plate 46. *Detail of plate 45*

Plate 47. *Detail of plate 45*

Plate 48. *Detail of plate 45*

TRIUMPH OF CONSTANTINE, Arezzo (*detail of plate 74*)

Plate 49. *Detail of plate 45*

Plate 50. *Detail of plate 45*

Plate 51. *Detail of plate 45*

Plate 52. *Detail of plate 51*

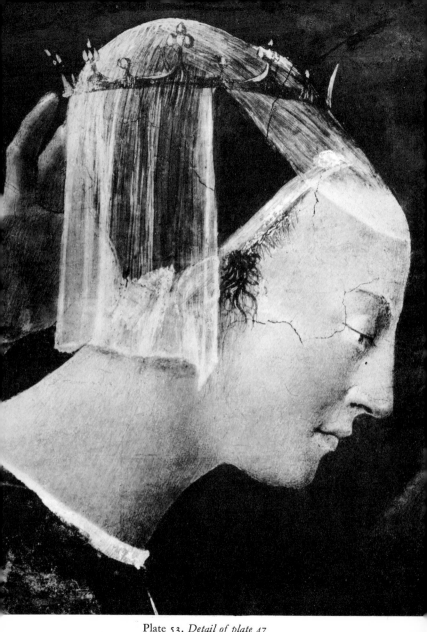

Plate 53. *Detail of plate 47*

Plate 54. SOLOMON RECEIVING THE QUEEN OF SHEBA, Arezzo

Plate 55. *Detail of plate 54*

Plate 56. *Detail of plate 54*

Plate 57. *Detail of plate 54*

Plate 58. *Detail of plate 56*

Plate 59. *Detail of plate 57*

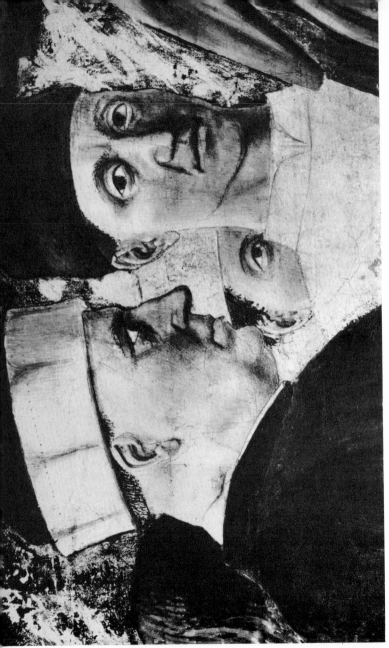

Plate 60. *Detail of plate 56*

Plate 61. *Detail of plate 55*

Plate 62. THE BURYING OF THE WOOD, Arezzo

Plate 63. *Detail of plate 62*

Plate 64. THE ANNUNCIATION, Arezzo

Plate 65. *Detail of plate 64*

Plate 66. *Detail of plate 64*

Plate 67. *Detail of plate 64*

Plate 68. *Detail of plate 64*

Plate 69. *Detail of plate 67*

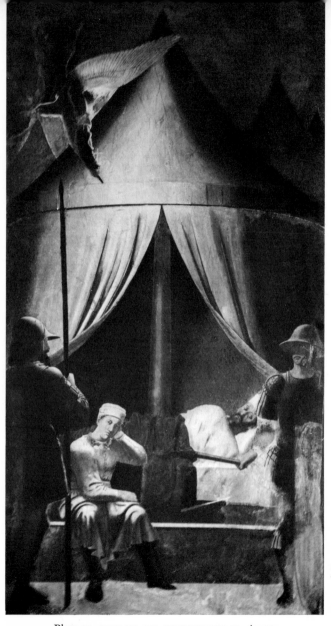

Plate 70. DREAM OF CONSTANTINE, Arezzo

Plate 71. *Detail of plate 70*

Plate 72. *Detail of plate 70*

Plate 73. *Detail of plate 70*

Plate 74. TRIUMPH OF CONSTANTINE, Arezzo

Plate 75. *Detail of plate 74*

Plate 76. *Detail of plate 74*

Plate 77. *Detail of plate 75*

Plate 78. *Detail of plate 74*

Plate 79. *Detail of plate 74*

Plate 80. *Detail of plate 78*

Plate 81. *Detail of plate 78*

Plate 82. *Detail of plate 74*

Plate 83. TORTURE OF THE JEW, Arezzo

Plate 84. *Detail of plate 83*

Plate 85. *Detail of plate 83*

Plate 86. THE DISCOVERY AND PROOF OF THE CROSS, Arezzo

Plate 87. THE DISCOVERY OF THE CROSS, Arezzo

Plate 88. *Detail of plate 87*

Plate 89. *Detail of plate 86*

Plate 90. *Detail of plate 87*

Plate 91. *Detail of plate 90*

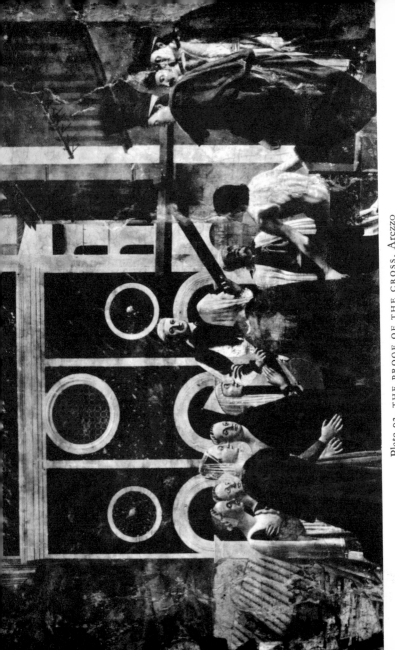

Plate 92. THE PROOF OF THE CROSS, Arezzo

Plate 93. Detail of plate 92

Plate 94. *Detail of plate 92*

Plate 95. *Detail of plate 92*

Plate 96. *Detail of plate 94*

Plate 97. *Detail of plate 93*

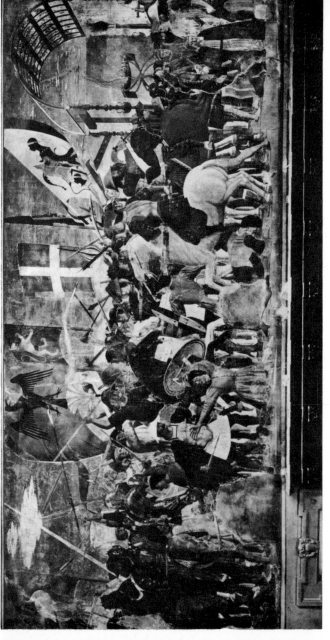

Plate 98. DEFEAT OF CHOSROES, Arezzo

Plate 99. *Detail of plate 98*

Plate 100. *Detail of plate 98*

Plate 101. *Detail of plate 98*

Plate 102. *Detail of plate 98*

Plate 103. *Detail of plate 98*

Plate 104. *Detail of plate 98*

Plate 105. *Detail of plate 98*

Plate 106. EXALTATION OF THE CROSS, Arezzo

Plate 107. *Detail of plate 106*

Plate 108. *Detail of plate 107*

Plate 109. *Detail of plate 107*

Plate 110. *Detail of plate 107*

Plate III. *Detail of plate 106*

Plate 112. *Detail of plate* 111

Plate 113. *Detail of plate 111*

Plate 114. PROPHET, Arezzo

Plate 115. PROPHET, Arezzo

Plate 116. ST AUGUSTINE, Arezzo

Plate 117. FACES OF ANGELS AND HEAD OF ANGEL, Arezzo

Plate 118. ST PETER MARTYR, Arezzo

Plate 119. ST LUKE THE EVANGELIST, Rome

Plate 120. ST MARY MAGDALEN, Arezzo

Plate 121. *Detail of plate 120*

Plate 122. RESURRECTION, San Sepolchro

Plate 123. *Detail of plate 122*

Plate 124. *Detail of plate 122*

Plate 125. *Detail of plate 122*

Plate 126. HERCULES, Boston

Plate 127. SAINT, San Sepolchro

Plate 128. ST AUGUSTINE, Lisbon, *and* ST MICHAEL, London

THE DISCOVERY OF THE CROSS, Arezzo (*detail of plate 86*)

Plate 129. SAINT, New York, *and* ST NICHOLAS OF TOLENTINO,
Milan

Plate 130. *Detail of plate 128*

Plate 131. *Detail of plate 129*

Plate 132. LOWER SECTIONS OF ST AUGUSTINE POLYPTYCH,
New York and Washington

Plate 133. MADONNA AND CHILD ENTHRONED, Perugia

Plate 134. SS ANTHONY OF PADUA AND JOHN THE BAPTIST,
Perugia

Plate 135. SS FRANCIS AND ELIZABETH, Perugia

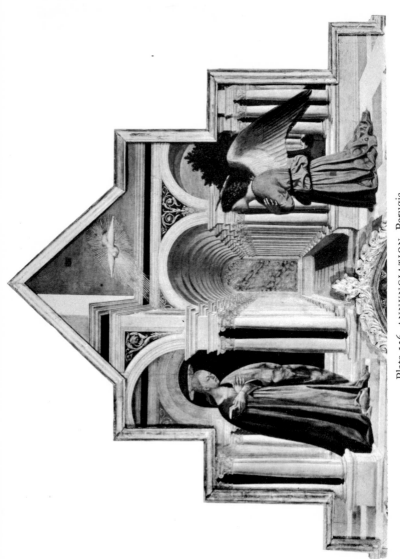

Plate 136. ANNUNCIATION, Perugia

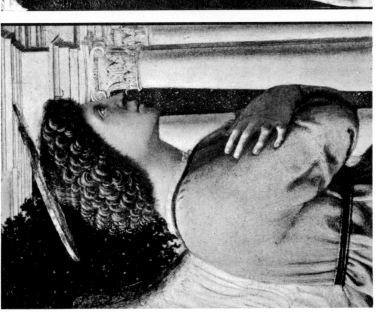

Plate 137. *Detail of plate 136*

Plate 138. ST CLARE *and* ST AGATHA, Perugia

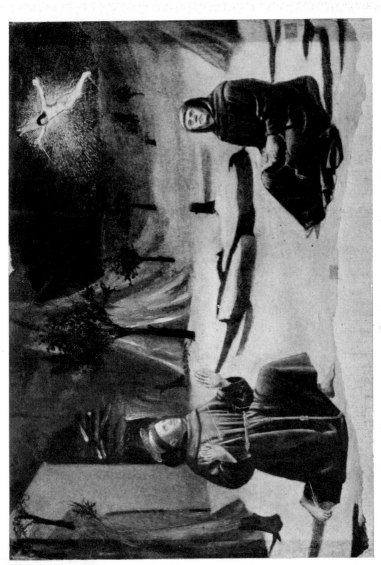

Plate 139. STIGMATIZATION OF ST FRANCIS, Perugia

Plate 140. ST ANTHONY PERFORMING A MIRACLE, Perugia

Plate 141. ST ELIZABETH PERFORMING A MIRACLE, Perugia

Plate 142. PORTRAIT OF BATTISTA SFORZA, Florence

Plate 143. PORTRAIT OF FEDERICO OF MONTEFELTRO, Florence

Plate 144. *Detail of plate 142*

THE SENIGALLIA MADONNA, Urbino

Plate 145. *Detail of plate 142*

Plate 146. *Detail of plate 143*

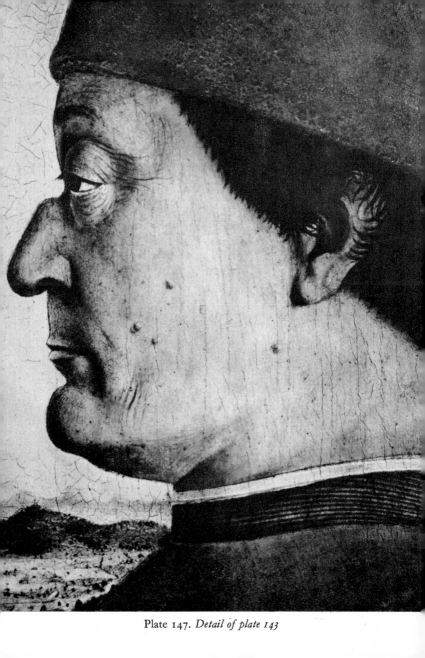

Plate 147. *Detail of plate 143*

CLARVS INSIGNI VEHITVR TRIVMPHO ·
QVEM PAREM SVMMIS DVCIBVS PERHENNIS ·
FAMA VIRTVTVM CELEBRAT DECENTER ·
SCEPTRA TENENTEM

Plate 148. THE TRIUMPH OF FEDERICO OF MONTEFELTRO,
Florence

QVEMODVM REBVS TENVIT SECVNDIS ·
CONIVGIS MAGNI DECORATA RERVM ·
LAVDE GESTARVM VOLITAT PER ORA ·
CVNCTA VIRORVM ·

Plate 149. THE TRIUMPH OF BATTISTA SFORZA, Florence

Plate 150. *Detail of plate 148*

Plate 151. *Detail of plate 149*

Plate 152. MADONNA AND CHILD WITH FOUR ANGELS,
Williamstown

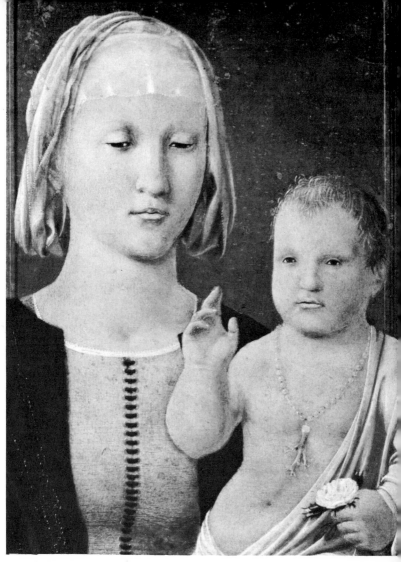

Plate 153. THE SENIGALLIA MADONNA (*detail of color plate IV*)

Plate 154. *Detail of color plate IV*

Plate 155. *Detail of color plate IV*

Plate 156. NATIVITY, London

Plate 157. *Detail of plate 156*

Plate 158. *Detail of plate 157*

Plate 159. *Detail of plate 156*

Plate 160. *Detail of plate 156*

Plate 161. *Detail of plate 156*

Plate 162. THE BRERA ALTARPIECE, Milan

Plate 163. *Detail of plate 162*

Plate 164. *Detail of plate 162*

Plate 165. *Detail of plate 162*

Plate 166. *Detail of plate 164*

Plate 167. *Detail of plate 165*

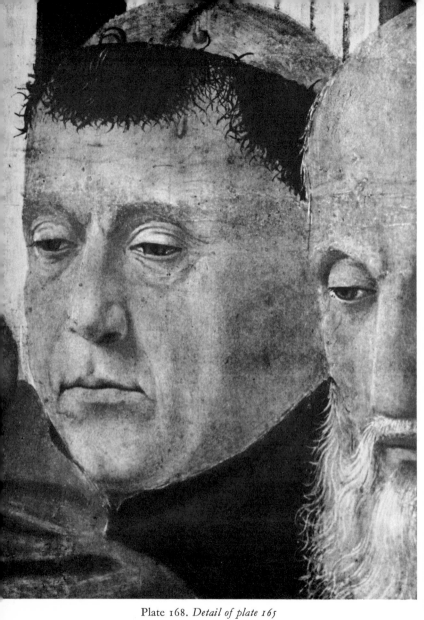

Plate 168. *Detail of plate 165*

Plate 169. *Detail of plate 165*

Plate 170. MADONNA AND CHILD, Florence (*attrib.*)

Plate 171. STUDY IN PERSPECTIVE, Florence (*attrib.*)

Plate 172-3. ARCHITECTURA

PERSPECTIVE, Urbino (*attrib.*)

Plate 174. SIGISMONDO PANDOLFO MALATESTA, Florence (*attrib.*)

Plate 175. ST LUDOVIC, San Sepolchro (*attrib.*)

Plate 176. THE VILLAMARINA MADONNA, Rome (*attrib.*)